Korea's Online Gaming Empire

Korea's Online Gaming Empire

Dal Yong Jin

The MIT Press
Cambridge, Massachusetts
London, England

For information about special quantity discounts, please email special_sales@ mitpress.mit.edu

This book was set in Sabon by Toppan Best-set Premedia Limited. Printed and bound in the United States of America.

Library of Congress Cataloging-in-Publication Data
Jin, Dal Yong, 1964–
Korea's online gaming empire / Dal Yong Jin.
     p.   cm.
Includes bibliographical references and index.
ISBN 978-0-262-01476-2 (hardcover : alk. paper) 1. Internet games—Social aspects—Korea (South) 2. Internet games—Economic aspects—Korea (South) 3. Video games industry—Korea (South)—History. I. Title.
GV1469.17.S63J56   2011
338.4'77948095195—dc22

                                                                    2010008161

10   9   8   7   6   5   4   3   2   1

Contents

I

Political Economy of the Online Game Industry

1

Introduction

Too often I hear people say 'South Korea' and 'emerging market' in the same sentence," said Rich Wickham, the global head of Microsoft's Windows games business. "When it comes to gaming, Korea is the developed market, and it's the rest of the world that's playing catch-up. When you look at gaming around the world, Korea is the leader in many ways. It just occupies a different place in the culture there than anywhere else. (Schiesel 2006, 1)

Online gaming has grown rapidly around the world over the past several years. While many countries—from those in the West, such as the United States, the United Kingdom, France, and Canada, to developing countries, including China, Taiwan, and South Korea (hereafter Korea)—have initiated modern information technologies and telecommunications networks, a few Asian countries, including Korea and China, lead the world in the development of online games. Unlike other cultural products, such as film and television programs, for which Western countries have dominated the global market, a few Asian countries such as Korea and China compete with major Western software developers and publishers in the global market. Among these countries, Korea has shown impressive progress in the development of online game software—more so than any other country in the early twenty-first century. As the largest game sector, the sales of domestic online games had soared as much as 56%, from $2.24 billion in 2007 to $3.49 billion in 2009 (Korea Creative Content Agency 2009).

Korea's rapid growth in the online game market has been unique in terms of the growth of its domestic online game industry, the dominance of its local games in the global market, and the degree to which its youth culture is embedded in online gaming. Although Korea was a comparative latecomer to the Internet revolution and broadband services because Korea was not advanced in the development and adaption of

Internet-related businesses compared to the United States and other Western countries, the country soon recognized the significance of online game development to its information economy. The Korean game industry has played a substantial role in the global game market in the midst of the market's swift growth, and the trend is expected to continue in the near future.

In 2006, the global online game market was valued at $4.98 billion, and it is expected to be worth as much as $11.88 billion in 2011 (138% increase); the global console/handheld game market is expected to increase by only 31.4% during that period. Asia constituted 49% of the global online game market in 2006, and Korea was the largest and most viable market in the world (PriceWaterHouseCoopers 2007). Although there are several video game sectors, including console, handheld, arcade, and, more recently, mobile sectors, the online sector has been the largest part of the video game industry in terms of growth. Korea has the highest percentage of broadband subscribers of any country in the world, and online gaming is the dominant segment of the game market there, unlike in Western countries, including Japan, Western Europe, and the United States, where console games dominate.[1]

Since the early twenty-first century, online gaming has become a massive cultural phenomenon, both domestically and globally, establishing itself as a huge Internet-based leisure activity and a popular and expanding form of entertainment in Korea's domestic market, with people continuing to spend more money and time playing online games. Korea has developed and pioneered several areas of online gaming, from software development to eSports (electronic sports and its leagues), which is the next stage of development in the online game sector. Playing online games involves active socializing and intertwined relationships; this is why the current generation is called the *game generation*. Gaming has moved beyond being merely a leisure activity—it is a social and cultural phenomenon (Ryu 2008).

The rapid growth of the online game market has changed the daily lives of many Koreans, particularly for young people in their teens and twenties who have used new technologies to nurture friendships and construct tight-knit communities through engagement in online games, instant messaging, blogging, facebooking, and the like in the Web 2.0 era. The broader populace in Korea is only starting to realize that gaming itself is not trivial but has become another channel of human relationships and part of people's lives (Lee, D. 2006). With the ever-increasing presence of online games in Korean mainstream culture, the corresponding consequences of games eclipsing other activities have also garnered much attention in recent years. Gamers in Korea have repeatedly made world headlines with reports of their perceived pathological use of games. The controversies have revolved around the compromise of real-life social activities due to addictions to the game, at home and especially at Internet cafés known as *PC bangs* (Jin and Chee 2009). (*Bang* means "room" in Korean.) The development of the online game industry and culture has become a primary sociocultural force in changing Korean society and the communication sector.

Korean Online Game Culture

With Korea's global presence and its domestic dominance in the online game industry, online game makers, online gamers, government information technology (IT) officials, and game researchers worldwide have been interested in examining the rapid growth of the Korean online game industry. With the immense popularity of online gaming and related industries, academic discourses on these topics are burgeoning from several perspectives, particularly from a cultural studies point of view (Chan 2008; Consalvo 2007; Wark 2007; Chee 2006; Whang 2003). To date, the academic research on Korean online games has been sparse and limited in scope, with Korea's domestic literature tending toward either a celebratory emphasis on positive business development or a focus on the problems of regulation and media-effects-oriented concerns (Jin and Chee 2008). As Terra Nova—the first Weblog of virtual worlds, beginning in 2003—shows, most academic studies of online gaming have focused on cultural discourses, emphasizing cultural influences of games and daily activities of general gamers. While such research contributes to the emergent scholarship on Korean online games, cultural discourse accounts tend to readily foreground the empirical observations and aggregate data to the exclusion of other possible macro factors, such as political economy structuration and transnationalization of Korea's local gaming industry and market. Conversely, due to rapid transnationalization and globalization, some researchers are skeptical of Korea's ability to compete with other countries, including China, in the next generation of online games, which means it is critical to understand the online game industry from not only a cultural perspective but also from political economy and globalization perspectives.

Previous studies have ignored or resisted critical inquiry into the online game field, although games constitute a new world that is, in terms of its social structure and economy, a real and viable alternative to the terrestrial world in terms of its social structure and economy (Castronova (2001), cited by Gunkel and Gunkel (2009)). Previous works also have not reflected on how the changing political economy environments in Korea and internationally have influenced the swift growth of the online game industry over the last two decades. With only a few works examining the genre of online games, and a vast majority uncritically celebrating this part of the industry, the critical study of online games mainly underserves the rapidly expanding field of knowledge (Leonard 2006).

Only a few works explore the socioeconomic meaning of online games and their associated industries. As Aphra Kerr (2006a, 4) states, "online gaming is a socially constructed artifact that emerges from a complex process of negotiation between various human and non-human actors within the context of a particular historical formation. Online gaming cannot be understood without paying attention to the late capitalist economic systems from which it emerged and the changing political, social and cultural contexts in which its commodities are produced and consumed." Ken McAllister (2004) argues that the game industry is much more than just software; it requires factory labor, large manufacturing plants, and massive distribution systems. The online game industry is even more than that because it is not a production-only business. Unlike the console, mobile, PC, and arcade game sectors, the online game sector extends beyond its institutional structure and system to areas such as professional game players, loyal fans, globalization, and broadcasting.

Several studies (Dyer-Witheford and Sharman 2005; Kline, Dyer-Witheford, and de Peuter 2003; Grimes 2006; Grimes and Feenberg 2009) have focused on the expansion of production processes into digital play, such as game workers and commercialization. However, little attention has been paid to the formulation of a critical political economy of online games that would allow for a broader understanding of several emerging areas, such as professional gamers, the commodification of online game fandom, and the globalization of online games. This book draws upon a range of theoretical perspectives and insights from media theory, such as the political economy of media, cultural studies, and globalization, to provide insight into the world of online gaming, both as a reflection of the complexity of online games and to uncover the political economy development of the Korean game industry and its ongoing reconfiguration. One of the fundamental perspectives applied in this book is the study of the development of the Korean online game industry based on the tradition of critical political economy.

Several media critics, including Dan Schiller, Robert McChesney, and Vincent Mosco, have analyzed the structural transformation of the media and telecommunications industries, and these analyses will be the major theoretical resources for a study of the online game industry. The rise of the communication industries, including the online game industry in the twenty-first century, led business to examine the economics of communications. The political economy of communication examines the nature of the relationship between media and communication systems and the broader social structure of society. As Dan Schiller (1996, vii) argues, the study of communication is not only to be concerned with the contributions of a restricted set of media; "the potential of communication study, in short, has converged directly and at many points with analysis and critique of existing society across its span." More specifically, Robert McChesney (2000, 2008) emphasizes that "the political economy of communication is a field that endeavors to connect how media and communication systems and content are shaped by ownership, market structures, commercial support, technologies and government policies." Vincent Mosco (2009a, 2–3) defines the political economy of communication as "the study of the social relations, particularly the power relations, that mutually constitute the production, distribution, and consumption of communication resources, including communication resources (such as newspapers, videos, films, and audiences)." Mosco also claims that political economy should broaden its meaning beyond the standard definition by focusing on a set of qualities that characterize the approach; "political economy has consistently placed in the foreground the goal of understanding social change and historical transformation."

As these media scholars argue, the political economy approach of studying the communication industry and, of course, the online game industry, should focus on the process of the structural and historical change of the communication system. The communication system is part of the broader socioeconomic arrangement. It is important to examine Korea's online game industry in the context of its political and economic systems. In addition, the Korean online game industry should be analyzed from a political economy approach because, in the twenty-first century, the industry has been the leading sector of Korea's capitalist economy and it has become a central part in the economic system. The Korean online game industry is large enough to be spotlighted in terms of its market volume and technological development; it is already a battleground for transnational corporations and is increasingly a part of a global game market. The major role of the political economy of communication is to analyze and be critical of the corporate communications system and the relationship between governments and media in a corporate capitalist society (Jin 2010).

Political economists of the media have also paid much attention to audiences, a major research category in previous cultural studies and now a part of the online game business in terms of how they are constructed and sold to advertisers as commodities (Smythe 1977, 1981; Jhally 1987; Artz 2008). Several media scholars criticize the lack of an analytical framework in the political economy of media for audience commodification. Political economist Dallas Smythe has guided a serious theoretical framework for analyzing audiences in relation to the commodification process.

Moreover, as Aphra Kerr (2006a, 7) argues, playing online games resembles work. Amateur game players and online game fans put a lot of work into playing and modding, or modifying, online games; leveling up their avatars; learning the codes and conventions; finding cheats; practicing; participating in online communities; beta testing games; and developing new characters or maps. Because this book critically analyzes online game fan culture and the fans themselves, as well as professional online game players in terms of the commodification process, the political economy of media provides a relevant and meaningful framework in understanding consumption. Nicholas Garnham (2000, 39) argues that political economy focuses on how power operates in the capitalist system, on its effect on the structure and performance of the media system, and on the relation between the producers and consumers of culture; this critical theory is therefore appropriate to analyze online gaming, which is a cutting-edge media product in our digital economy.

This book considers the game industry to be a main sector of the economic system. To understand the changing game industry, one must examine it as a core business of highly capitalized corporations. This book uses a political economy approach to investigate the relationship between online game industries and the broader society and to address the relationship between the growth of eSports and government policy, which includes the production, distribution, and consumption of cultural products.

This book uses other theoretical frameworks as well; in particular, it examines the Korean online game industry through the lens of globalization. While many Western game companies are rapidly investing in the Korean market, several Korean game developers, such as Nexon and NCsoft, have expanded their influence into the global market.

Because this book examines several new topics in the field of online gaming, including eSports, professional game players, new labor workers, globalization, online game fan culture, and audience commodities, and because several theoretical frameworks are used in these examinations, each chapter describes the framework selected to examine its particular topical area.

Korea's Reorganizing Game System

This book examines the multiple causes of growth of the online game industry in Korea. First, this book explains why and how the Korean government adopted new economic and cultural policies to develop the online game sector as a cutting-edge business and cultural icon. Second, it examines the role of Korean and foreign-based transnational corporations in the online game industry. It discusses whether transnational corporations have played a significant role in the reorganization of the new media structure, especially with respect to online gaming, over the last ten years. The relationship between international transnational corporations and Korean-based transnational and national corporations will also be examined. In this light, the book discusses the impact of neoliberal globalization on the game industries and on government policy. Third, this book explicates the nature of the relationship between online game systems and the broader structure of Korean society, examining the pattern of ownership and production in the game industries and analyzing these patterns within the overall context of social and economic power relations.

Finally, the book articulates whether the apparently flourishing online game corporations in Korea will continue to thrive. Despite experiencing dramatic growth over the last decade, the Korean online game industry is now stagnating, due to increasing competition from other countries. Korean online games have experienced shrinking shares in the global role-playing market due to the rapid growth of rivals—in particular, online games from China in recent years. In addition, console makers in Japan and the United States continue to expand their share in one of the most active game markets, Korea. This book discusses the next challenge of Korea's local cultural industry, which plans to maintain and/or expand its global presence by developing new games, as well as improving global–local strategies.

The goal of conducting a political economy analysis of the Korean communication industry is to allow game and media scholars, government communication policy makers, and IT experts around the world to better understand the reorganizing game system of Korea and shed light on the shifting global game industry.

Political Economy as a Methodological Framework

Media scholars and game researchers still have difficulties defining the field of online gaming and finding appropriate theories and methodologies to study it because online games entered public consciousness in a relatively short period of time, and even more rapidly within Korea (Jin and Chee 2008). The majority of qualitative analysis on the gaming industry has been derived from cultural studies, built upon the work of Raymond Williams (1974). Similarly, much scholarly analysis and discourse argue that online games can be understood not only as texts but also as cultural artifacts that are given value, meaning, and position through their production and use by game players (Crawford and Rutter 2006). Several of those studies, using various methodologies, have focused on the cultural aspects of online games, such as identities among youth and changing lifestyles in cyberspace in the development of online game identities in Korea (Chee 2006; Whang 2003). Other studies analyze social issues, including game addiction and content controversies (Jeon 2004; Kim et al. 2006).

Though the body of academic research on games using various methods of examination has grown rapidly, online gaming has received scant attention from political economists (Dyer-Witheford and Sharman 2005). Such examinations from a political economy perspective would complement existing games research, lending an additional understanding to the practices associated with gaming and to the conditions of such emergent cultural practices. As Toby Miller (2006, 6) has advocated, digital games scholarship needs to attend to its medium's political economy. He states that "every cultural and communications technology has specificities of production, text, distribution, and reception." The online game industry is no longer a discrete sector. Its circuits, technology, culture, and promotion have become intertwined with the wider orbits of a digital capitalism betting on digital networks as the critical zone for growth and profits (Kline, Dyer-Witheford, and de Peuter 2003, 176). The field would benefit from discussions of the economic, technological, and cultural implications of the new digital technology. That does not mean that all scholarly work should use both approaches in understanding online games. Instead, it argues that online game theory and methodology must be a synthesis of a wide range of approaches as a multidisciplinary field of research (Wolf and Perron 2003, 13). Thomas Malaby (2006, 151) confirms that "one of the most important features of online games is the way the costs of producing or distributing them are transformed, and this should be an important avenue for future research." Indeed, a complementary structural examination provided by a political economy approach seems to fit the demand expressed by such cultural researchers of online game phenomena.

As Daniel Miller and Don Slater (2000) point out in their critique of Manuel Castells' (1996) work on the political economy of the Internet, there is a difficulty in covering political economy and ethnographic approaches; however, online games have to be defined based on specific combinations of technical, social, cultural, and economic characteristics and not on exclusive, and essential ones (Raessens 2005, 373). In this regard, while emphasizing the importance of the Asia-Pacific region as one of the most distinct and growing online game markets globally, Larissa Hjorth and Dean Chan (2009) articulate the importance of the integration of industry, culture, and politics in the emerging local game industry in Korea. Through an examination of the Korean online game industry in light of its sociocultural elements and political economy contingencies, this book illuminates some of the underexamined complexities inherent in the conception, development, implementation, and reception of online games in a global arena. Alongside the mix of diverse theoretical perspectives, this hybridized methodological framework contributes much to moving research and inquiry forward in gaming studies, the public sphere of popular criticism, state and private policy creation, social movement critique, and labor organization. This allows "us to consider who makes the games, who profits from them, how they target audiences, what the games look like, what they are like to play, and how they fit in with social life" (Miller 2006, 8).

This book combines political economy approaches with in-depth interviews of online game fans, online game team managers, and online game cable television workers conducted in Seoul, Korea, between June 2007 and January 2009. Primary and secondary resources, such as industry reports and government documents, were combined with observation of everyday life in Korea, Korean *PC bangs*, and interviews with game players to show the manifestations of policy and culture as experienced on the ground, especially by Korean youth.

Organization of the Book

As background to the rapid growth of the online game industry, chapter 2 describes Korea's shifting political economy in the post–International Monetary Fund era and its move toward an IT-driven economy. The chapter examines the roles of the government and competition among telecommunications companies in developing broadband services, which served as a foundation for the growth of the online game industry in Korea, and attempts to ascertain the causes of the rapid growth of broadband services in the context of broader sociocultural factors. The chapter recognizes technology as a sociocultural product and explores elements contributing to the diffusion of broadband services in the context of the cultural environment in Korea. Furthermore, it discusses the significant role of Korean people, as users, in the process of the rapid diffusion and growth of broadband services.

Chapter 3 investigates the rapid growth of the Korean online game industry. Korea's software developers have been able to outperform major foreign competitors, such as EA, Blizzard Entertainment, and several Asian online game developers, including Shanda in China. In this chapter, the Korean game industry is analyzed with regard to its own sociocultural circumstances and context in relation to the global game industry. Factors involved in the swift growth of online games in the context of broader sociocultural elements are identified and examined. The chapter provides a critical interpretation of the industry's ownership patterns, finance, and markets by exploring online games and the industries developing in Korea. It describes the forces driving development by examining government policies and competition among online game companies.

Chapter 4 discusses the development of eSports. eSports was originally used as a narrow definition of electronic sports leagues that competed through network games. With the growth of online games, the notion of eSports has expanded to include not only competition through network games but also cultural and industrial activities related to network games. Although Australia first started eSports with Nintendo games, eSports instituted its first league in 1998 when the game *StarCraft* became popular in Korea. eSports then became one of the major activities among youth in their teens and twenties; the live broadcasting of competitions on cable TV networks has expedited the growth of online games, particularly among mainstream Korean youth. The chapter investigates the role of eSports in the growth of the online game industry and professional game players. Finally, it discusses the reasons that cable and network broadcasters are so heavily invested in eSports by focusing on the convergence of telecommunications and broadcasting.

Chapter 5 studies professional online game players, who are unique to Korea. In Korea, where visual culture and new media are growth industries, professional online game players have quickly gained popularity among the youth, and their cultural influence on young people should not be overlooked. This chapter uses a Marxian analysis of commodification to examine the working conditions of professional gamers as labor workers to determine their professional identities. Because the major focus is to analyze the professional online gamers as new media workers, the chapter elaborates on whether the professional gamers' world is full of existing labor issues, such as exploitation of workers as commodities and the existence of gendered environments. It maps out the commodification process of professional gamers, a practice that is due largely to the hardships endured as part of professional game teams that are owned by media, telecommunication, and other big corporations. Finally, it asks whether professional gaming—the combination of youth, talent, and culture in online gaming, as in new media work—is a viable future for youth representing current media workers in the digital economy.

Chapter 6 analyzes the commodification process of online game fans. As Dallas Smythe argues, the audience's relationship and interaction with the media acts as a continuum from the audience's entertainment to the advertiser's commodity. The audience is not simply passing time; it is spending time in regimented ways with advertising-supported media as the focus of attention or as the focus of socializing. The relationship between professional game fans and professional teams can be described in similar terms. The game fans' participation in online game shows and fan club meetings is commodified and marketed as both a paid-for leisure experience and as a key selling point of corporations having game teams. More importantly, audience members buy goods and spend their incomes accordingly. Corporations owning online game teams clearly understand what they sell to ever-increasing audiences that represent all socioeconomic classes: not only goods and services but also their brands. The most important thing for them is that audiences get used to their brand name. The chapter discusses the ways in which companies owning professional game teams have benefited from the convergence of technology, culture, and youth, not only in production but also in consumption. More specifically, it describes how corporations such as those involved with telecommunications, media, and online publishers have deliberately organized this convergence as part of their marketing strategies, which has resulted in a new audience commodity process.

Chapter 7 describes the shifting trend of globalization with the case of online gaming, because the success of Korea's local online games as a genre in the global market has arguably become a unique case of contracultural flow. In this chapter, the globalization process of Korea's local online game industry is discussed with the case of the *Lineage* games, which are massively multiplayer online role-playing games (MMORPGs) released in 1998 and 2003, respectively, and which have rapidly increased their level of dominance in the global online game market. The chapter discusses the ways in which Korea's local online game industry has produced a global phenomenon. The goal of the chapter is to trace the production dynamics to identify the conditions that have rendered contracultural flow possible. It discusses the process by which a local culture is appropriated for a global audience. Finally, the chapter articulates whether this contracultural flow demonstrates that an asymmetrical cultural flow exists in favor of non-Western countries, and, in particular, that the United States' dominance has diminished. It illuminates some of the underexamined complexities inherent in the conception, development, implementation, and reception of online games in a global context.

Chapter 8 examines the structural transnationalization of the online game industry. The online game industry has rapidly involved itself in transnationalization as a reflection of the convergence of content and capital, which has resulted in much faster transnationalization than in, for example, the film industry. This chapter examines recent trends of transnational corporations' engagement in the online game industry, to ascertain whether these trends confirm that transnational corporations play pivotal roles in the cultural market. The major focus is on capital flow and on people and financing, meaning the chapter is meant to describe how the online game industry has developed its transnationalization in several ways to fully understand the nature of the transnationalization process. It also articulates whether emerging online game firms, as part of the new cultural industry in non-Western countries, have changed the traditional interpretation of the global flow by blurring the dichotomy of the West and the East. This inquiry leads to questions of whether the transnationalization of the online game industry has promoted the shift of traditional interpretations of cultural dominance by Western countries in the global market in the midst of globalization.

2

Sociocultural Interpretations of Digital Korea

Introduction

The rapid deployment of high-speed Internet (broadband services) throughout the world has changed the social and technical landscape of cyberspace remarkably. Broadband services have made it easier to download digital music and movies, and the wide penetration of broadband services has enabled customers to engage in online stock transactions. Worldwide, many schools, from elementary schools to universities, are connected to broadband services and utilize IT for education. Internet broadcasters have become popular. In particular, broadband services have become a major factor for the growth of online games, primarily because always-on and high-speed connections are required for online game businesses and culture. Many countries—both developed and developing countries—have initiated modern telecommunications networks that support broadband access to homes and offices to develop the social and technical landscape of cyberspace (Han 2003; Ishii 2003; Lee and Lee 2003). As of December 2008, about 95% of Korean households were connected to broadband services, the highest percentage in the world; connection rates were much lower in Canada (76%; 9th), the United Kingdom (67%; 14th), Japan (64%; 16th), and the United States (60%; 20th) (Strategy Analytics 2009).

Consequently, Korea has become the world's best example for the adoption of broadband services—and a place to look for answers on how the Internet business, including online gaming, may evolve (Taylor 2006). Much scholarly analysis and discourse (Lee, O'Keefe, and Yun 2003; Reynolds and Sacks 2003; Choudrie and Lee 2004; Lau, Kim, and Atkin 2005; Lee, Oh, and Shim 2005; Jin 2005; Lee, Kim, and Yongtae

2009) has focused on the roles of the government and competition among telecommunications companies in developing broadband services in Korea. These studies emphasize several factors contributing to the rapid growth of broadband services caused by the deregulation and competition in the telecommunications sector, such as policies to promote Internet use and the strategies of broadband service providers. Previous studies, however, have not paid much attention to sociocultural factors, which are one of the most important contributing elements. Although a few papers do examine cultural factors that contribute to the use of broadband services, their discussions are not comprehensive.[1]

This chapter explores the causes of the rapid growth of broadband services in the context of the broader sociocultural elements of Korean life to determine important factors for the growth of the online game industry and market in Korea. It recognizes the adoption of new technology as a sociocultural phenomenon; the chapter explores cultural elements contributing to the diffusion of broadband services in the context of the cultural environment in Korea. Furthermore, it discusses the significant role of users in the process of the rapid diffusion and growth of broadband services. In particular, it emphasizes the way in which the 1997 economic crisis, one of the most significant sociocultural turning points in modern Korean history, influenced the deployment of broadband services.

Technology as Cultural Form

It is generally recognized that technologies are primarily neutral from a moral standpoint, because they operate under the same norm of efficiency in all situations. Many users of technology argue that technology is amoral and an entity devoid of values (Rescher 1969; Mesthene 1970). In fact, throughout the history of technological innovation, its main architects have often denied their moral responsibility. This instrumental theory, the dominant view of modern governments and the policy sciences on which they depend, argues, "if people use technology for destruction or pollution, as in the case of nuclear weapons and chemical pollution, it should not be blamed on technology, but on its misuse by politicians, the military, big business and others" (Pacey 1983, 2).

For many scholars, however, technology is not simply a means to an end—it is an environment and a way of life; this is its substantive impact (Borgmann 1984). This theory of technology holds that technology is not neutral but has a substantive value bias. Substantive theory, best known through the writings of Jacques Ellul, Arnold Pacey, and Martin Heidegger, claims that technology constitutes a new type of cultural system that restructures the entire social world as an object of control. For instance, Heidegger (1977, 17) claims that technology is relentlessly overtaking us. People are engaged, he claims, in the transformation of the entire world, ourselves included, into "standing reserves," raw materials to be mobilized in technical processes. Substantive theory explicates cultural aspects of technology, such as values, ideas, and the creative activity of technology (Feenberg 1991). This type of cultural system is characterized by an expansive dynamic, which ultimately mediates every pretechnological enclave and shapes the whole of social life.

Jacques Ellul (1964) states that one must examine technology through its sociological aspects: "we should consider the effect of technique on social relationships, political structures, and economic phenomena." Technology is not aloof from the social realm; on the contrary, it is an integral part of the social (Webster 2002). Arnold Pacey (1983, 4–6) also discussed how those who write about the social relations and social control of technology should be made aware of the cultural aspects as well as the organizational and technological aspects.

Cliff Christians (1989, 124–125) observes, "technology is the distinct cultural activity in which human beings form and transform natural reality for practical ends with the aid of tools and procedures." He clearly argues that cultures are humans' distinctive and immediate environment built from the material order by men and women's creative effort. Furthermore, Raymond Williams (1992, 127–129) stated, "how technology develops is not only a matter of some autonomous process directed by remote engineers, but is a matter of social and cultural processes." Technologies are developed and used within a particular social, economic, and political context (Franklin 1999). As these theoreticians emphasized, technology does not develop independently but is part of a particular social, economic, and cultural process. This chapter contributes to this ongoing debate of substantive theoretical discourse with a case study of the rapidly growing use of broadband services in Korea.

Institutional Factors in the Growth of Broadband Services

The rapid deployment of broadband services in Korea began in 1995 when the government enacted the Framework Act on Information, which established the first Master Plan for setting up a comprehensive strategy for the Korean Information Infrastructure (KII) (Ministry of Information and Communication 2004).[2] The goal of the KII was to construct an advanced nationwide information infrastructure consisting of communications networks, Internet services, application software, computers, and information products and services (Jeong and King 1997). The KII project aimed at building high-speed networks by providing over 80% of households with over 20 Mbps (megabits per second) of broadband access by 2005 through market competition and private sector investment (Lee, O'Keefe, and Yun 2003). Because household penetration of broadband services was recorded at more than 95% at the end of 2008, the government achieved one of the major goals of the KII; however, the speed of broadband, another major goal, was not fulfilled. The average speed of high-speed Internet in Korean households was less than 20 Mbps in 2008. Broadband service providers plan to invest $1.3 billion in 2008 and 2009 to upgrade the speed to 100 Mbps by 2010, because they need super-speed broadband services for daily use of Internet Protocol television and Internet telephone, which are emerging new media areas. As a result, LG Powercom and SK Broadband have upgraded the speed to 100 Mbps starting in April 2009 (*Chosun Ilbo* 2008; *Naeil News* 2009).

In Korea, endeavors to develop high-speed Internet services were accelerated after the 1997 financial crisis. The financial crisis severely affected the Korean economy due to unprecedented rates of unemployment, massive-scale corporate bankruptcies, and the substantial decline of the stock market. The economic situation demanded that Korea change its industrial structure, from traditional heavy and chemical industries to a more IT-oriented structure based on telecommunications and computers. More importantly, Korea identified IT as its path to economic recovery following the 1997 financial crisis (Kim, P. 2006). The Korean government deployed a high-capacity backbone and pursued a policy of high-speed telecommunications infrastructure as a foundation for IT changes required for sustainable economic growth (Lee, O'Keefe, and Yun 2003).

Under these circumstances, government planning and stable funding played significant roles in the rollout of broadband services. The Korean government invested $11 billion in broadband services between 1998 and 2002, while the U.S. government planned to invest only $2 billion in the form of tax breaks as of May 2003 (Belson and Richtel 2003, C1). The Korean government also introduced a variety of promotion policies expediting the growth of broadband services, such as creating Internet-friendly classrooms[3] and Ten Million People Internet Education, which was to enhance Internet literacy through a number of IT educational programs. The government set up several training programs in which 10 million people such as the disabled, housewives, and those in military service would attend a variety of programs by the end of 2002 (MIC 2002). Korea's rapid and expansive broadband growth can be traced, in large measure, to government initiatives (Lau, Kim, and Atkin 2005, 351).

Competition among telecommunications corporations also greatly contributed to the deployment of broadband access throughout Korea. Broadband services in Korea were first introduced in 1998, and telecommunications companies, including Korea Telecom (KT)—the largest telecommunications company in Korea—Thrunet, and Hanaro Telecom, fiercely competed for high-speed Internet market share. In May 1999, Thrunet, the corporation that introduced broadband services to Korea, held 63% of the market share, followed by Hanaro Telecom (35%) and KT (2%). The market has undergone substantive change in recent years; KT has become the largest player in the broadband market since its privatization in the early twenty-first century.[4] Hanaro Telecom, controlled by U.S. investors American International Group Inc. and Newbridge, absorbed Thrunet in late 2005 to better compete with KT. LG Powercom, a subsidy company of the LG group, entered the market in September 2005, and several cable system operators have expanded their shares in the high-speed Internet market (Kim, D. 2006). As a result, as of March 2008, KT had 48% of the market share, followed by Hanaro (23%), LG Powercom (14%), and others (Kim, J. 2008).[5]

The intense competition among telecommunications companies led to price (monthly fee) reductions and subsequently a rapid increase in demand for broadband services (Jin 2005). Prices decreased from $40 per month in April 1999 to $30 in February 2003, and again to less than $20 in May 2006 (International Telecommunication Union 2003a; Taylor 2006), although the price bounced back to $37.81 in October 2007. At the same time, the average monthly subscription price was $53.10 in the United States, $59.80 in Canada, and $41.10 in Japan (Organization for Economic Cooperation and Development 2008). These relatively low monthly subscription fees have helped the growth of broadband services; however, a high subscription fee would likely not have deterred the spread of broadband services in Korea because the majority of Koreans weigh other factors besides price in deciding whether to purchase a subscription. Sociocultural characteristics of Koreans also play key roles in the Korean use of broadband services.

Korea has been developing the next generation of high-speed Internet services. Acknowledging the existence of market saturation, it has enhanced the capacity of existing broadband services, including speed and convergence with various types of media, such as Internet telephone. Again, the Korean government and service providers have tried to upgrade the speed of broadband to 100 Mbps to promote use of Internet telephone, movies, Internet Protocol television, and online education (*Chosun Ilbo* 2008). Furthermore, Korea expects the rapid penetration of 100 Mbps broadband services will expedite the growth of image-related content and online game businesses, bringing a second wave of high-speed Internet services in ten years.[6] As such, the Korean government and telecommunications companies play a pivotal role in the growth of broadband services by providing infrastructure, government initiatives, and market competition.

Social Factors Contributing to the Diffusion of Broadband Services

While the Korean government and telecommunications companies played significant roles in the deployment of broadband services, the phenomenal growth of broadband services would not have been possible without consumers who rapidly accepted and adopted the new technology. Several social elements such as *PC bangs*, online stock trading, and online games have played significant roles in the growth of broadband services in Korea because they have shaped and influenced people's daily lives.

PC bangs were a necessary element in generating the Internet boom and the swift deployment of broadband services, because many Korean users, especially young people, were first exposed to high-speed Internet access in Internet cafés. The *PC bang* later played a crucial role in shaping and forming the sociocultural context and business for Korean online gaming (Huhh 2009, 103). *PC bangs* offer 24-hour-a-day access to the Internet to the public through leased lines; they are equipped with multimedia computers and offer high-speed access to the Internet at almost $1 per hour in late 2002, and $0.73 per hour in 2007 due to severe competition among *PC bangs* (Korea Game Industry Agency 2008). *PC bangs* have since evolved as places for Koreans to send e-mails, chat, research information, and so on at any time of the day or night (Lee, O'Keefe, and Yun 2003).

The popularity of online stock trading also prompted the growth of broadband access. Online stock trading is one of the most significant social phenomena in Korea since the 1997 financial crisis. During the economic crisis, the Korean stock market almost collapsed. The composite Korea Stock Price Index plummeted from 1050.93 on July 9, 1997, to 770.84 on October 22 of the same year, and it fell to 498.42 on December 5, 1998 (Korea Stock Market Company 1999). After the 1997 financial crisis, the number of individual stock investors soared from 1.32 million in 1997 to 3.97 million in 2002, accounting for 8.3% of the total population (*Korea Times* 2001; Korea Stock Exchange 2002). These individual stock investors held 35.5% of total listed shares and accounted for 97.2% of online trading through broadband services. Therefore, some 67% of all stock trading was done online by the end of 2002, compared with 10% in 1998 (*KyungHyung Shinmun* 2002).

Stock investors need broadband services, not only because it provides always-on connections and high speed, but also because it makes it possible to check the results of their trading instantly and cheaply. In addition, stock investors could stay at their homes or offices with high-speed Internet instead of visiting stock companies for their transactions. Many individual stock investors first used *PC bangs* for their online stock trading in the late 1990s before they began to subscribe to broadband services at home (Jin 2010).

Finally, an increase in the demand for entertainment and online games has stimulated the diffusion of broadband services in Korea. According to a survey conducted in June 2003, about 47% of broadband subscribers said that they used broadband services primarily for online games, followed by movies and television programs (37.4%) and community activities (23.6%) (*Economic Review* 2004). For instance, the online game *StarCraft*, developed in the United States, contributed to the rapid growth of broadband connections and Internet cafés beginning in 1998. *StarCraft*, in which players are competing with other netizens through a network, became one of the most popular online games, and, again, many Korean students visited Internet cafés to play the game, and later the *Lineage* games. Because broadband service providers and online game developers acknowledged the clear relationship between broadband and online games, some companies started to sell new packaged services. For example, SK Broadband and NCsoft, the largest online game developer and publisher in Korea, agreed to provide a free card to play *AION*, NCsoft's new MMORPG, for a year when people subscribe to broadband services (SK Broadband 2008).

In addition, the Korean culture played a role in the growth of broadband services, in that Korean people are not familiar with monthly payment systems for games, unlike game users in Western countries. Many online game players were introduced to online games at and continue to go to *PC bangs* to enjoy games with hourly charges. Several online game companies, including NCsoft, have contracted with *PC bangs* to attract users. *PC bangs* pay license fees to online game companies (*Economic Review* 2004). The rapid growths of *PC bangs* and online gaming go hand in hand in the Korean context.

Against this backdrop, it is crucial to understand the historical influence of the 1997 financial crisis, because *PC bangs* were first introduced during the economic crisis by workers who had been laid off from major electronics companies or by owners of small software companies whose businesses went bankrupt (Aizu 2002). Before and after the crisis, several large conglomerates, including Daewoo, went bankrupt. When they failed, more than three thousand mid-size and small companies collapsed, and many workers lost their jobs. By the end of June 1999, the number of unemployed reached 1.78 million, the highest number in 13 years (Jin 2010). Employees laid off during the economic crisis were the main participants in Korea's growing Internet industry. Many middle managers who had worked for large computer and information companies turned to small private businesses (Rohwer 2000). Many of them joined Internet start-ups and became grassroots developers of Internet technologies, including online games software, and others started their own small businesses, including *PC bangs.*

For these workers, Internet cafés were one of the most attractive new businesses, because they were not expensive to operate (Rohwer, Chowdhury, and Kraar 2000). In 1997, there were only 100 *PC bangs* in Korea, but they rapidly increased with the growth of broadband services and became popular, with approximately 3,000 in 1998 and 23,548 in 2001. Although the number of *PC bangs* decreased with the increase in the number of home computer users, there were still as many as 20,607 in 2007 (Korea Game Industry Agency 2008). With over 20,000 *PC bangs* and with professional game players, as discussed in chapter 5, Korea has been lauded as an example of how gaming can become mainstream (Hjorth and Chan 2009). *PC bangs* have also been a strong revenue source for online game corporations. For example, half of NCsoft's $12.2 million in revenue in 2001 ($6.1 million) came from *PC bangs*, followed by individual users (35.5%). With the rapid penetration of broadband access in households, individual users have become the largest revenue sources for online game publishers since 2002; *PC bangs* are the second largest revenue source (NCsoft 2009a; Huhh 2009).

PC bangs, which might be called a by-product of the Korean financial crisis, have contributed to the growth of online game corporations. Many people play online games, including *StarCraft*, *Lineage [I]* and *II*, and *AION* at *PC bangs*. Aspects of *PC bang* culture may be likened to arcade gaming in the late 1970s and 1980s. As in many other countries, arcade games were the most popular game genre in Korea until the rapid growth of online games in the mid-1990s with the growth of personal computer (PC) use. Several arcade games, including two famous games, *Galaga* (a fixed shooter arcade game) and *Tetris* (a puzzle game), were popular with Korean youth in the 1980s. Starting in the late 1990s, *PC bangs* became a kind of offline playing field for computer gaming where people could enjoy playing online games with their friends face to face (Huhh 2009).

StarCraft, one of the most popular online games, had a crucial role in the growth of *PC bangs*. With the advent of Blizzard Entertainment's *StarCraft* in 1998—a real-time computer strategy game with networked multiplayer capabilities that proved to be an early success and was a contributing factor in the mass popularization of network computer games (Chan 2008)—young people were quick to abandon popular leisure activities, including arcade games, en masse. Christian McCrea (2009, 179) observed that Korea and *StarCraft* were locked in a symbolic relationship. *StarCraft* was originally published by a division of LG Electronics, LG Soft, in Korea as a contractor of Blizzard Entertainment. Because of the financial crisis of 1997, the company was forced to downsize. A managing staff member of LG Soft at the time, Young-man Kim, made a bold decision to establish a new game start-up based on *StarCraft* named HanbitSoft. The first thing that HanbitSoft did was to distribute free copies of the game at the newly proliferating *PC bangs*. At that time, *PC bangs* were a focal point among the young who could not find their first jobs and the unemployed who had been sacked due to widespread corporate downsizing (Huhh 2009, 306–307). In short, several social factors became drivers for the phenomenal growth of broadband services, which allowed for the rapid development of online game businesses and culture.

Cultural Attributes Contributing to the Deployment of Broadband Services

While many countries around the world have initiated and supported the growth of broadband services, the result varies markedly due to the acceptance of new technology by the users, as well as government initiatives—not all countries have had Korea's success. Clearly, there are unique cultural characteristics that make Korea a broadband empire. The swift growth of broadband services would have been impossible without people readily accepting new technology. The diffusion of services and the widespread use of high-speed Internet took place with rapid acceptance by most Koreans, not only teenagers but also older people.

Therefore, it is crucial to explore the significance of assessing the culture in which technology is created and the context in which it is widely accepted. As the International Telecommunication Union acknowledges (International Telecommunication Union 2003b), Internet user demand contributed most decisively to the rapid explosion of broadband in many places, particularly in Korea. Again, Jacques Ellul (1964) emphasized, "the development of technology is not an isolated fact in society but is related to every factor in the life of modern humanity." Cultural specificities embedded in Korean history—in particular, the 1997 economic crisis—should be emphasized as significant factors that prompted the rapid deployment of high-speed Internet. A few additional cultural characteristics in Korean society aided in the swift deployment of high-speed Internet services, including enthusiasm for "edutainment," and a comfort level with both social solidarity and individualism.

The primary Korean cultural characteristic that expedited the growth of high-speed Internet was a demand for quick change. Only a few decades ago, Koreans were characterized as calm and patient, as one distinguished Confucian characteristic, but, in just a few years, the demand for quick change became one of the most distinctive Korean characteristics (Han 2003, 19). Since the 1960s when the country began its high-speed transition from an impoverished state to one of Asia's major economies, Koreans have become less patient. Korean society is well known for its impulsiveness; that is, its desire for quick communication, quick contact, and quick results (Jin 2010). Korea is nothing if not dynamic. In this regard, Jong Suk Lee (2000), director of the Korea Culture and Policy Institute, states, "nine out of ten Koreans rush into the road as soon as the light changes to green and they cross the street on or even before the green light is about to turn red. In contrast, Chinese would usually wait until all the traffic is cleared and safe even at the clear green light. And if the light is about to turn red, they just stop and wait for the next green light." Indeed, *balli, balli*—Korean for "hurry, hurry"—is heard incessantly on the crowded streets of Seoul, reflecting the frenetic pace of Korean life in a global era (Jin 2010).

A survey conducted in the 1980s is still compelling—according to the survey (Chinese Cultural Connection 1987) on Confucian dynamism, which measures long-term versus short-term orientation, Japanese residents received one of the highest scores, compared to residents of the United States, the United Kingdom, and Australia. The high Japanese score in the survey reflected the patience or long-term orientation of Japan compared with other developing countries (McFadyen, Hoskins, and Finn 1998).

This relentless drive, which has led Korea to chalk up a number of achievements, has also driven the spread of broadband Internet connections. Most Koreans have hurried to have broadband Internet connections, and it has been easier to expand these services compared with other countries, including Japan. Most Koreans want quick communication, quick games, and quick contact. Everything needs to be *balli, balli*, and this mentality has expedited the rapid deployment of broadband services. For most Koreans, everything needs to be done right now. For example, in Korea, instant messaging is comparatively popular because not answering a message from a friend with all due speed is considered a faux pas in Korean society (Taylor 2006).

Korea is full of early adopters who are willing to buy newly released digital devices for consumer testing. In a survey by Korean ad agencies in 2004, 43% of respondents said that they consider themselves early adopters in the market (Kwon 2006). According to a survey by the U.S. market research firm Parks Association in November 2005, Korea ranked second on the list of thirteen countries in the adoption of consumer technologies (Parks Associates 2005).[7] Although *balli balli* culture has several negative aspects, such as bribery scandals and the collapse of buildings and bridges, including Sungsu Grand Bridge in 1994 and Sam-Poong Department Store in 1995, in the midst of achieving social and economic successes in the Korean society, rapid adaptability to change is important for the swift deployment of broadband services.

An enthusiasm for edutainment—the combination of education and entertainment—has also greatly contributed to the unique growth in broadband services in Korea. Korea is one of the most developed countries in terms of education. Its overall school enrollment rate (primary, secondary, and tertiary) of 90% is the highest in the world. Korea's high rates of literacy and school enrollment are essential as prerequisites for the widespread adoption of information and communication technologies (ICTs), and these factors have helped contribute to the growing impact of ICT in Korean society (International Telecommunication Union 2003a). Overenthusiasm for education in Korea is not new, but, after the 1997 economic crisis, Internet skills were considered to be one of the most important survival tools for many Koreans. They devoted their attention to the Internet as a necessary technology for their jobs, education, and entertainment (Jin 2010). In particular, for most parents, broadband is a necessary tool for children's education. Relatively simple initiatives such as encouraging schoolteachers to post homework assignments on their own Web sites and requiring students to submit their assignments by e-mail creates a feeling among parents that the Internet is a necessity for their children's education (Choudrie and Lee 2004).

In particular, during the economic crisis, parents started to realize the potential threats and opportunities of globalization. It became a must for their children to acquire both English and Internet skills in order to survive in the era of globalization (Aizu 2002). Many Korean parents with young children have focused on online English education since the late 1990s. They have acknowledged that their children are able to enjoy online reading, music, games, and animation written in English through the Internet due to high-speed connections and 24/7 support services as an alternative to learning English in a classroom. In the Korean context, the need for education has also developed edutainment as a form of studying English while enjoying playing in cyberspace (An 2001).

Edutainment is not only for children. Many workers in their mid-careers have also turned their focus to the Internet in the midst of a changing working environment. In Korea, the majority of companies have adopted a Western-style five-day workweek (instead of the previous six-day workweek), starting in the late 1990s and early twenty-first century. The spreading five-day workweek has boosted IT, such as DVDs, mobile games, and edutainment. With more spare time available, people began looking for a new type of education containing more entertainment factors, instead of cramming (Cho 2002). Therefore, having high-speed access to the Internet at home became an advantage, benefiting everyone from children to housewives to career persons, and it became a disadvantage if one did not have it. Broadband is indispensable for edutainment, which is one of the major contributing factors in the rapid adoption and growth of broadband services.

At the same time, the Korean *me-too culture*, which means companies and people tend to end up with the same systems and taste, has substantially contributed to the spread of broadband access. People in many countries are susceptible to social pressure to keep up with their neighbors; however, Koreans' willingness to keep up with their peers is relatively much higher. Koreans tend to be early adopters of technology, and they are fast followers, as Stephen Ward, consultant manager of the telecommunications group at Deloitte observed. Koreans are conscious of the need not to be left behind by others, and the young have a great desire to conform with the gadget-carrying norm of their peers (Ward 2004). The majority of Koreans believe businessmen should get the same salary if they begin the job in the same company at the same time, and parents have difficulty accepting the fact that their children are left behind relative to others. Koreans feel they must be in the best position in terms of the quality and quantity of their houses, education, and income. Many Korean people buy new refrigerators when their neighbors buy them, and they buy pianos when their neighbors buy them, although they have refrigerators and pianos good enough to use.

Likewise, many Koreans are eager to have high-speed Internet because they want to keep up with their neighbors. They feel that if they have the service, they could be part of the group; if not, they might be left out of the group. Technology and fashion fads tend to spread like wildfire in Korea. If one individual adopts an innovation, then others feel a social pressure to follow (Bajaj 2002; Lau, Kim, and Atkin 2005). The me-too culture works in broadband services. Many old and new apartments are installing broadband Internet connections because the construction companies and apartment complexes do not want to be behind other apartment buildings (Han and Jung 2006). The me-too culture has contributed to the rapid deployment in broadband services.

On the flip side, the me-too culture represents another aspect of Korean culture, known as *mass play culture*, which has become a crucial element for the growth of online gaming. People do not want to be left out by not working and/or playing together. In the realm of video games, unlike young people in the United States who want to play as single players with or without other players online, Korean young people do not like to play alone; they prefer to be part of teams that defeat other teams. As will be discussed in detail in chapter 7, the mass play culture characterizing Korean society has been a major factor in the popularity of *Lineage [I]*; NCsoft has adopted single-player modes for *Lineage II* in order to attract young American players. Sociocultural aspects are certainly significant factors for the growth of both broadband services and online gaming in Korea.

Finally, the younger generation has played a crucial role in the rapid deployment of high-speed Internet. Korea is a country that is proud of its tradition of social solidarity (Crotty and Lee 2002). People do not want to be left out. The *New York Times* reported in 2002, "Korea is a group-oriented society, where socializing in bunches is the preferred form of interaction, and Western-style individualism is frowned upon," while reporting on booming online games (French 2002, 8). After conducting a case study of online games in Korea, Florence Chee (2006) also emphasized the importance of social solidarity of teens and those in their twenties in the process of growing online game communities. The flourishing of online communication matched the culture and emotion of the Korean people and their need for communication with one another through boards—forums to discuss and exchange information—and clubs, which brought together people with similar hobbies (Seong 2006).

However, this conventional wisdom has changed in recent years, and individualism—the degree to which individuals are able to achieve identity and status on their own rather than through membership in groups (McFadyen, Hoskins, and Finn 1998)—is on the rise in Korea. In this regard, the *New York Times* did not reflect on the rapidly changing environment in Korea. With the swift change in the economy before and after the 1997 financial crisis as well as recent modernization, Korea's social and cultural situation has shifted on a large scale. The younger generation increasingly seeks Western culture, regarding an individual's success, private property, and nuclear family as important, instead of the value of the Confucian culture emphasizing patriarchy and large extended families. According to a marketing report by SK Telecom, "those in their 20s and 30s, the first Internet generation in Korea, gives priority to their own time and space, rejecting all invasions of privacy. They are also changing the culture of collectivism to one of individualism" (*Joongang Ilbo* 2002, C3). The double personality of many Koreans—on one hand embracing social solidarity and on the other hand embracing growing individualism—has contributed to the rapid growth of broadband services. As Florence Chee (2006) observes, young people enjoyed popular online games sometimes with friends and other times alone, but always through high-speed Internet. While seeking social solidarity, many young people enjoy high-speed cyberspace by creating their own worlds, and this changing sociocultural characteristic has become crucial for the rapid growth of high-speed Internet in Korea.

In sum, the explosion of broadband access in Korea has been possible due in large part to various cultural factors, rooted deeply in Korean society and its historical context, in particular the 1997 economic crisis.

Korean citizens are the most significant component of broadband service diffusion because they are the main users of the service. Without high-speed Internet, Koreans could not have a normal sociocultural life, including enjoying individual cyberspace, from online games to edutainment, in one of the fastest growing information societies. This quick pace accelerated after the 1997 financial crisis because many Koreans began to realize that speedy change and adoption of new IT was necessary to survive in a globalized world. As Izumi Aizu (2002) points out, the social and cultural factors, the attitude of the Korean people, high awareness of the challenges of globalization, and political and historical contexts played the decisive role in its dynamic acceptance of Internet and acceleration to broadband in Korea.

Summary

Korea's rapid deployment of broadband services in the degree to which broadband service penetration has been achieved is unique. Several important factors have contributed to the rapid deployment of broadband services. The government and telecommunications companies, as providers, have played important roles in the rapid development of broadband Internet; in particular, providing infrastructure for its development. Favorable government policies and competition among telecommunications companies became driving forces for the rapid deployment of broadband Internet.

The explosion of broadband access in Korea, however, was made possible against the backdrop of the 1997 economic crisis and due to various deeply rooted social, historical, and cultural factors. Although political factors can be important driving forces behind broadband penetration, growth also requires an existing receptiveness to using the services and applications that can be provided through broadband. In this regard, it was the Korean citizens who made inroads into the world's most receptive market for broadband services.

Several sociocultural factors, which are crucial to the diffusion and use of new technologies, have played significant roles in the swift deployment of broadband services in Korea. Cultural characteristics emphasizing speedy communication and enthusiasm for edutainment have contributed to the exponential growth of broadband services. The growing complexity of characteristics of the younger generation (showing comfort with social solidarity and individualism, something that is not easy to find in any other country) has particularly contributed to the rapid growth of broadband services. If the younger generation had only one of these two characteristics, the characteristic would not have contributed as greatly to the rapid growth of broadband services. In the midst of globalization that was expedited with the economic crisis in 1997, the younger generation has developed unique characteristics that resulted in one of the most significant cultural factors in broadband Korea. The majority of Koreans have been eager to gain new technologies, and their unique cultural characteristics have become an important component in the rapid deployment of broadband services.

In conclusion, the introduction and development of new technology cannot be explained solely in terms of political structures and economic policy surrounding technology. As Jacques Ellul (1964) stated, "one should be looking at technology in its sociological aspect because technology is not an isolated fact in society but is related to every factor in the life of modern man." Technology does not develop independently but is part of a particular social, economic, and cultural setup. The deployment of broadband services in Korea has been possible due to its specific sociocultural dimensions, as well as the political and economic environment. Cultural characteristics rooted in Korean society have greatly influenced the growth of technology, broadband services, and, later, online gaming throughout the country.

3

Political Economy of the Korean Online Game Industry

Introduction

The Korean online game industry has become one of the most dynamic in the world. While several countries (both Western and non-Western) have rapidly invested in the online game industry and have become involved in the development of online games, Korea has played a central role in the PC-based online game market and digital economy since the late 1990s. Ever since Nexon, a Korean games developer, introduced the world's first graphic MMORPG with *The Kingdom of the Winds* in 1996, Korean game corporations have developed immensely profitable and skillfully designed online games, including *Maple Story*, *Lineage [I]*, *Lineage II*, and *AION*, which have made Korea an online game empire. The industry's vibrancy is obvious, and, for Korea's online game companies, life seems easy—as if operated by a joystick (Kim 2009). Primarily due to the rapid growth of users, and the structure and dynamics of the interactive game business, the Korean online game industry has become a key node in the networked environment of virtual capitalism (Kline, Dyer-Witheford, and de Peuter 2003, 169).

There are several contributing factors for the growth of the online game industry in the Korean context, including favorable government policies, a competitive market structure, a swift development of ICTs, the transnationalization and globalization of the game industry, and people's mentalities about accepting new technology and online gaming. The online games development industry in Korea continues to be supported by extensive government intervention and preferential cultural industry policies (Chan 2008, 189). The fundamental growth of the online game industry has also been made possible through the swift development of ICTs. The online game market is being driven by the increase in broadband subscribers, although a transition to the next generation of consoles has gradually occurred since both Sony and Microsoft introduced online gaming capabilities through their consoles (Chan 2008; PriceWaterHouseCoopers 2007).

Globalization and transnationalization are also fundamental factors for the growth of the online game sector. Over the last decade, many foreign-based game giants, such as Blizzard Entertainment, Electronic Arts (EA), Microsoft, Nintendo, and Sony have swiftly invested in the Korean game market in the midst of neoliberal globalization. In the 1990s, the U.S. government and international agencies such as the IMF and the World Trade Organization pushed non-Western countries, including Korea, to open their media and telecommunications markets, such as film, broadcasting, and telecommunications industries. Since the online game industry became a new media area, and the government had already opened the new media market, including cable and mobile sectors, transnational corporations (TNCs) easily penetrated the Korean online game market with their advanced capital and marketing skills. Consequently, the Korean online game market has been a battleground between foreign-based TNCs and Korean-based TNCs since the early twenty-first century, which has resulted in the growth of Korea's local game industry. Along with the rapid growth of broadband and the ascent of *PC bangs*, several other factors, such as the popularity of *StarCraft* and the 1997 economic crisis, also affected the rapidly changing online game system. These historical events played significant roles in establishing the online game industry as a primary part of Korean society and culture.

It is worthwhile to analyze the context of the rapid growth of Korean online games, because contextualization provides a process for connecting present circumstances to the social and historical conditions from which online games originated. Several key factors involved in the rapid growth of online games in the context of broader socioeconomic elements are explored; more specifically, this chapter critically examines several significant aspects of the industry's ownership patterns, the market structure, and financing of the online game industry. It maps out the forces driving its development by examining government policies and competition among online game companies. In particular, it addresses the major role that the government has played in the development of IT, which includes the online game sector. Finally, this chapter provides a historical account of how the online game industry has contributed to the diffusion of online games in the socioeconomic milieu specific to Korea. This chapter also sheds light on current debates of neoliberal transformation in the global video game industry and its culture.

The Emerging Korean Online Game Market

The video game market, as it relates to consumer spending on console, handheld, PC, mobile, and online games—referring to games carried out on a computer network—is a burgeoning new media industry with global revenues rivaling those of film and music (Dyer-Witheford and Sharman 2005; Carr et al. 2006). Between 2001 and 2005, the worldwide game market increased by about 30%, to $27.1 billion. It is expected that the game market will increase from its 2007 figure of $41.9 billion to $68.3 billion in 2012, growing at a 10.3% compound annual rate (Price-WaterHouse Coopers 2006, 368; 2007, 424; 2008, 404). As is well chronicled in media reports, the primary driver of the global game market is the growth of console games, where gamers play on a dedicated console, like Sony's PlayStation 3, Microsoft's Xbox 360, and Nintendo's Wii. These major console producers and service providers, which have provided game platforms and/or devices, have dominated the global video game market in an oligopolistic contest. In the United States, console games, including handheld games, constituted 74.4% of the market at $8.64 billion in 2007. The situation is not much different in Europe (60.6%), although online games are growing (PriceWaterHouse Coopers 2008). Although there are other game areas, including online and mobile, due to the rapid growth of the console game sector, advertisers are turning to games as a means of reaching the male 18-to-34-year-old demographic. Therefore, the total amount of advertising on video games has soared from $30 million in 2004 to $1,044 million in 2007 (PriceWaterHouse Coopers 2008, 419).

In contrast to this trend in many Western countries, online games have been markedly in vogue and are playing a critical role in Korea's systematic transformation toward a digital economy and culture. The online game platform allows players to download games and game content to compete against others via the Internet. The PC platform is traditionally the only means by which to play games online, and it is still the dominant platform, although both Sony and Microsoft introduced online gaming capabilities through their consoles in 2002. For instance, Xbox Live offers game downloads, video chat sessions, and the ability to compete against other players online. While there is a free version of the environment, which has limited capabilities, the majority of players pay $50 annually as of 2007 to enable full access and to allow them to compete against other players around the world (PriceWaterHouse Coopers 2007, 432).

The growth of online gaming has been phenomenal in the Korean context. In 2000, for example, sales in the domestic gaming industry were valued at $1 billion, and online gaming only accounted for 22% of the game market. During the same year, as a reflection of the dominance of arcade games before the rapid growth of online games, arcade games were the largest game genre (60%), and PC games were the third at 13%, while mobile (3%) and console games (2%) were marginal (Feller and McNamara 2003). However, only a few years later, in 2005, the Korean online game market accounted for as much as 76.2% ($1.4 billion) of the total game market ($1.89 billion), and this figure accounted for 56% of the entire Asia-Pacific market share. During 2005, the console game market constituted only 11.5%, followed by mobile games (10.3%), and PC games (2%) in Korea. The online game market rapidly increased by as much as 41.3% between 2004 and 2005 (Korea Game Industry Agency 2006). Korean online games, as of March 2007, also made up 32% of the world's online gaming market (Kim 2007). For example, in Thailand, Korean games accounted for 80% of the market, and the situation is similar in Vietnam and the Philippines as of June 2009 (Choe 2009). The Korean online game market grew and recorded $2.8 billion in 2008. In 2010, it is expected to be $3.9 billion (Korea Game Industry Agency 2008).

The most popular online game genre has been the MMORPG; however, there are several more online game genres becoming more popular among young people, including casual games, first person shooter games (FPS), and sports games (golf, soccer, and car racing). In fact, after the introduction of *Lineage II* in 2003, several game firms diversified their genres, from MMORPGs to casual games (e.g.,

KartRider) and FPS (e.g, *Special Force* and *Sudden Attack*), to expand their revenue sources while avoiding any financial risk from the potential failure of one or two major games, particularly MMORPGs, because this game genre needs ample development costs. Due to their efforts to make new game genres and changing users' preferences, non-MMORPGs gradually extended their market share in the Korean game market. For example, during December 2008, five MMORPGs (including *AION*, *Lineage*, *World of Warcraft*, and *Maple Story*) still made the top 10 most popular online games list; however, casual (*KartRider*), FPS (*Sudden Attack*), and sports (*FIFA Online 2*) games also ranked in the top 10 (Cho 2009).

The Korean online game industry has also rapidly expanded its influence in the global market. In 2008, Korea exported $898 million, about a 15% increase from the previous year, in the gaming business (Korea Game Industry Agency 2008). When Korea exported $565 million worth of online games in 2005, the film industry exported $76, and the broadcasting industry exported $123.5 million in television programs, the two of which had been major cultural sectors leading to Korea's increasing cultural penetration in Asia (Ministry of Culture and Tourism 2006). The export of Korean films has rapidly decreased, from $76 million in 2005 to $24.4 million in 2007 (Korean Film Council 2009); the game industry, and particularly the online game industry in the Korean context, has started to outgross the Korean movie industry basis.

The largest foreign markets for Korean online games were traditionally in East Asia, including China, Japan, and Taiwan. In particular, China and Japan have been the two largest markets for Korean online games. In 2003, China accounted for as much as 62.1% of Korean online game exports, followed by Taiwan (16.5%). During the same year, the United States (5.7%) and Europe (2%) were smaller markets. However, there have been some significant changes since that time. While China has reduced its dependency on Korean online games, and Japan and the United States have become important markets, because Korean online games have rapidly penetrated these countries. In 2007, China and Japan each received 31% of Korean online game exports, followed by the United States (17.7%), Taiwan (7.7%), and Europe (5.3%) (Korea Game Industry Agency 2008, 53). The Korean online game industry also has a presence in Latin America, the Middle East, and Russia.

Chinese game companies quickly caught up to the Korean game industry in the area of online games in the midst of the Chinese government's support, which has resulted in a decrease of market share for Korean online games in China. However, Chinese developers still have a long way to go before they overtake their Korean rivals, because of soaring development costs and skills requiring sophisticated graphics and game structure (Rhee and Wei 2009). Therefore, the Chinese game market, alongside the Japanese market, will be the largest market for Korean online games, at least in the near future. *AION*, the most popular MMORPG after the *Lineage* games developed by NCsoft, for example, got a license contract with Shanda Entertainment—the Chinese game developer—for $50 million, which is the largest in the game industry. Korean online games are still dominant in China (Lee, N. 2009).

In fact, in the global game market, several of Korea's online MMORPGs and casual games have become popular. *KartRider*, which is an online car racing game developed by Nexon, has been played in 71 countries, including Russia and China, since 2004 (*JoongAng Ilbo* 2009). *Groove Party*, which is a stylish online dancing game with a brand-new concept that unites groovy rhythm and dynamic action, has been played in China with sales of $4.7 million. The casual online golf simulation game *Pangya*, developed by NTreev and published by HanbitSoft, was played in Japan, Thailand, Europe, North America, and Korea in 2009. Korean MMORPGs have been well received in many countries. *Maple Story*, an MMORPG produced by the Korean developer Nexon, boasts 15 million users nationwide and is available in 58 countries, serving 75 million users around the word as of August 2008 (Jeong 2008). NCsoft—the largest Korean online game developer and publisher—has particularly dominated the global online game market since it released its medieval fantasy MMORPGs, *Lineage [I]* and *Lineage II* in 1998 and 2003, respectively. The games were available in Chinese, Japanese, and English language versions and have been considered one of the largest commercial MMORPG communities before the emergence of *World of Warcraft*, developed by Blizzard Entertainment in the United States in 2004 (Mmogchart.com 2007). In fact, since 2005, *World of Warcraft* has become a dominant MMORPG in the Korean game market.

However, Korea's domestic game market has changed since NCsoft offered *AION* in November 2008. In October 2008, three major online games developed by Blizzard Entertainment (*StarCraft*, *World of War-craft*, *WarCraft 3*) consisted of 20% of games played in the *PC bangs* in Korea, while NCsoft's *Lineage* games accounted for 14% of the *PC bang* market. However, as of early January 2009, *AION* consisted of 19.1%, while *World of Warcraft* was only at 6.1% (Lee, N. 2009). *AION* also rapidly penetrated the global market, including China, North America, and Europe. For example, since launching its open beta service in China, *AION* has recorded more than 500,000 concurrent users as of May 2009, and Gamespot, an influential U.S. Web site for video and computer games, has *AION* ranked second only behind Blizzard Entertainment's *StarCraft 2* as the most anticipated game title of the year (Kim 2009).

In fact, as one can see in table 3.1, *AION* made $42.6 million worldwide during the first quarter of 2009, while *Lineage II*, which was the most lucrative online game for NCsoft, earned $41.1 million (NCsoft 2009b). As such, the Korean online game industry has developed several key games for global game users and commercialized online games in the global marketplace. Although there are several global game giants, including Blizzard Entertainment and EA, the Korean game industry has been one of the most vibrant in the global market, and Korea successfully promotes online games as a major part of its digital economy.

Table 3.1
Revenue Profile of NCsoft, 2004–2009

Game	2004	2005	2006	2007	2008	2009
Lineage	112,806	115,012	118,049	111,401	112,602	29,351
Lineage II	110,609	118,953	119,206	131,154	147,211	41,126
AION	—	—	—	—	9,682	42,649
City of Heroes/ City of Villains	31,475	34,265	25,016	23,446	24,218	6,837
Guild Wars	—	41,308	52,600	42,058	23,227	4,300
Others	—	—	2,052	6,356	9,507	1,730
Total	254,890	309,538	316,923	314,415	326,447	125,993

Note: The data are given in U.S. dollars ($1,000). The data for 2009 is for the first quarter (January–March).
Source: Data from NCsoft 2009a.

Structural Imbalances in the Online Game Industry

The creation of a video game can be divided into three distinct processes: development, publishing, and distribution. The development sector entails the design and creation of a piece of game software. This expensive process may be financed either through the developer's own funds or by venture capital, or, increasingly, by advances from a game publisher (Dyer-Witheford and Sharman 2005). Most Korean developers secure capital primarily from their own funds (29.7%), followed by publishers (21.3%), corporate investment (14.2%), and other methods (Korea Game Industry Agency 2008, 131). Publishing involves the overall management of the game commodity—financing, manufacturing, packing, and promotion of a game. Distribution refers to the shipping of the game hardware and software to retail outlets (Dyer-Witheford and Sharman 2005).

However, the game industry presents a rather complicated picture, because development, publishing, and distribution functions can be combined by one company or separated into two or three corporations. This is different from the music and film industries, where those functions are typically integrated into one production label. For games, a single company can perform just one or a combination of these three activities (Kline, Dyer-Witheford, and de Peuter 2003). Because of the difficulty in dividing the game industry, game-developing firms and publishing companies are lumped into the same category as development companies by the Korean government (Article 2, Law on Game Industry Promotion), unlike other countries that separate publishing from the development sector.

To begin with, the number of Korean online game firms has increased dramatically over the past several years. In 1999, when the Korean online game industry was in its infancy, the country had a total of 694 game companies. However, that number soared to 3,797 companies in 2005, although it slightly decreased to 3,744 in 2007. During the same period from 1999 to 2007, the number of game development companies, as the largest in the industry, increased 6.7 times from 416 in 1999 to 2,792 companies in 2007, while the number of distributors increased 3.4 times from 278 in 1999 to 952 in 2007 (Korea Game Industry Agency 2008). To offer a comparative perspective for a similar time period, Canada had only 247 video game companies, including both game developers and publishers, as of August 2008 (Entertainment Software Association of Canada 2009). This means that the Korean online game industry has witnessed phenomenal growth. Because the majority of Korean game companies often do not work exclusively on online games but also on mobile and offline PC games, it is unclear how many of them are actually online game companies. However, according to one survey, about 53.1% of game companies are reporting the production of online games, followed by mobile games (30.8%) in 2007 (Korea Game Industry Agency 2008, 119). These online game companies, ranging from major publishers and middle-sized companies to small developers, together produce approximately 100 new games every year (Chung 2008, 309).

With the rapid increase in the number of game firms, the number of employees in the game industry, including the mobile and online sectors, has also swiftly increased as a reflection of the popularity of game firms as a new workplace. Overall, the number of total employees soared from 23,594 in 2001to 60,669 in 2005 (table 3.2), far exceeding the number of workers in the media industry (40,116), including newspaper, terrestrial and cable broadcasters, and news agencies (Korea Press Foundation 2005). Because many game corporations develop for two or three game platforms at the same time (e.g., online and mobile), it is difficult to sort out the number of employees in the online game industry; however, again, 53.1% of game companies focus on online games as their major platform, so it is likely that the majority of game workers are part of the online game sector. The number of employees rapidly dropped to 32,714 in 2006, with some rebound to 36,828 in 2007, from 60,669 in 2005 (Korea Game Industry Agency 2008). The sharp drop was caused by the drastic shrink of the arcade game sector, whose revenue plummeted in the midst of a bribery scandal between late 2005 and early 2006. Nevertheless, this figure still exceeded several major countries, including Japan (30,000 in 2003), the United Kingdom (20,000 in 2002), and Canada (6,000 in 2005) (Kerr 2006b).

The Korean game industry has continued to show inequality between male and female workers in the workplace. Among game workers, about 79% of the employees are men, so the male workforce is three times larger than its female counterpart. The gender inequality also influences the characteristics of the work in the game industry. In particular, the male workforce has been dominant in certain major areas of the game

Table 3.2
Indicators of the Korean Online Game Market

Market Indicator	2001	2002	2003	2004	2005	2006	2007	2008
Domestic Market	191	452	754	1,018	1,439	1,777	2,243	2,756
Exports	130	141	172	368	565	672	78	898
Developing Companies	1,381	1,774	2,059	2,567	2,839	2,786	2,792	3,317
Number of Employees	23,594	33,870	39,104	47,051	60,669	32,714	36,828	42,730
Educational Institutions	—	44	62	82	69	71	75	71

Notes: Domestic market and export figures are given in U.S. dollars ($1 million). These figures are from the entire game industries, including online, PC, arcade, and mobile sectors. The figures of domestic market size are for the online game sector only. Online games consist of 95% of game exports. Education institutions include high school, junior college, universities, and graduate schools.
Sources: Data from Korea Game Industry Agency 2006, 2007a, 2008; Korea Creative Content Agency 2009.

industry; for example, in 2007 more than 90% of game producers were men (92.8%), alongside other major areas, such as computer programming (93%) and system engineering (92.5%), while female workers were associated with general secretarial positions (24.8%), marketing and PR (27.5%), and as scenario writers (21%) (Korea Game Industry Agency 2008).

The majority of Korean game companies are small in terms of the average number of employees as a reflection of the characteristics of the cottage industry. Game-developing companies had 28.7 employees on average in 2007, up from 22.5 in 2006. Compared to other media and entertainment industries, such as film and broadcasting, the game industry has a much smaller number of workers and assets. Of course, several major online game corporations, including NCsoft (1,300 employees), have more than 1,000 employees and have rapidly become cultural giants comparable to those in the film and broadcasting industries. With a few exceptions, the increase of employees per company in recent years has happened primarily because of mergers and acquisitions between companies, rather than because of the entrance of new game corporations.

The average salary in the game industry is not promising. The average salary in the U.S. game industry was $61,403 in 2001, and, depending on experience, programmers earned between $55,000 and $88,000 (Olsen and Zinner 2001). According to Game Developer magazine (2009), the leading video game industry publication, the average salary has continuously increased to $79,000 in 2008, a 7% increase from the previous year. While the recession is significantly impacting the number of jobs available in the United States, the income of still-employed game industry professionals in 2008 continues to edge up (Game Developer 2009). However, in the Korean game industry, the average salary of the 15 major game companies was $30,000 in 2008. Although some game workers in a few big online game corporations, including NCsoft, received about $39,000 on average, salaries in the second-tier game corporations, including HanbitSoft, ranged from $19,200 to $23,000 during the same year (This is Game.Com 2009). Because the majority of game workers have worked less than five years in their career, mainly between two and three years, this figure itself does not prove that game workers receive lower salaries than workers in other countries. However, given that most of the workers work more than eight hours a day, and about one-third of workers work until late at night at least four times per week, one might say that their overall salaries are not promising (This is Game.Com 2009).

Meanwhile, the online game industry has shown unbalanced market concentration. As in many other industries, such as film, television, and mobile technologies, a few of the largest game developers and publishers dominate the Korean game market, and the concentration of wealth in the industry has increased in recent years. Although there were about three thousand development houses, the top five online game companies, including NCsoft, Nexon, Neowiz, NHN, and CJ Internet, constituted 63% of the online game market in 2008 ($1.7 billion out of a total of $2.7 billion). This was up from 54% in 2006, which means that the Korean online game market is becoming an oligopoly with fewer than ten companies controlling the market (Seo 2009; Lee and Ryu 2006). The majority of game companies are small developers trying to maintain business by producing graphics, hosting Web services, and making simple board games (Chung 2008, 310). Among the top developers and publishers, NCsoft made its name with the launches of MMORPGs *Lineage* (1998) and *Lineage II* (2003), which offer players involvement in combat, sieges, and political and social systems. With the successful launch of *AION* in 2008, NCsoft is expected to maintain its status as the largest online game firm in Korea, while competing with global game giants. Nexon, the second largest developer, provided *The Kingdom of the Winds*—the first online game in Korea, followed by several successful games, including *KartRider* and *MapleStory*. These two top online game companies accounted for 62.5% of the top five online game companies in 2006 (Seo 2009). Resources such as capital, workforce, and technology are favoring a handful of leading game firms. As emphasized by Kline and others (2003, 177) and Dyer-Witheford (2004), the dominance of online games by a few major companies could continue indefinitely, because game development is an increasingly lengthy, costly, and cooperative venture. The escalation of production and marketing costs and the difficulties in recruiting skilled workers are persistent challenges to the majority of small game developers, which has resulted in a decline in their market share.

Indeed, the cost of developing one online game soared from $185,000 in 1999 to $10 million in 2008, and several developers have spent more than $30 million to develop MMORPGs. It also takes 100 workers about 2 to 3 years to create a big game in Korea (Park, D. 2008; M. H. Kim 2005). This means that small developers who have less capital and a smaller workforce cannot compete with the few largest game developers. For example, CJ Internet spent 31 months and $10 million on the production of its online role-playing game *PRIUS Online* (Park, D. 2008). Bluehole Studio, which is a new game developer, has been developing its first MMORPG, known as *TERA*, for three years starting in 2007, and the cost will reach $32 million (Shim 2009). Because game developers and publishers invest a lot of money in marketing as well, the online game industry is now doing blockbuster-style development. This situation will continue in the game development sector, as only a few venture capitalists and large corporations are able to manage the blockbuster-level scope of game development and production timelines. However, the online game industry is itself vulnerable because only a few block-buster titles dominate the market (Rhee and Wei 2009).

Meanwhile, structural imbalances in the online game industry continue because ownership is concentrated amongst a few large developers and publishers. Several major game companies have expanded their roles in the online game business as a way to compensate for the difficulties in financing and marketing experienced by the majority of developers (Jin and Chee 2009). Through vertical and horizontal integrations, several game corporations have tried to create synergy effects as seen in many other media and telecommunications industries. For example, in 2008, T3 Entertainment acquired 26.4% of the shares of HanbitSoft, and Dragonfly acquired Pantagram. NHN bought 10% of the shares of Webzen, and Nexon acquired 50% of the shares of Neople. HanbitSoft and Webzen were two of the largest online game developers; however, they could not manage their soaring developing costs and became victims of mergers and acquisitions (Ryoo 2008).

Firms involved in telecommunications, media, and international trade, such as SK Telecom, KT, CJ Internet, and LG International Corporation, have joined the emerging new media and technology sector in the hopes of another windfall. In 2008, SK Telecom acquired 51% of the shares of NTreev ($20 million), an online game developer, as part of a strategic plan to intensify its role in the media content area. In 2003, KT announced that it would invest $100 million in the games market over the next five years, as a publisher. Since then, KT has funded nine online games, including *Herrcot*, as of March 2005 as a publisher and actively exported games to other countries, such as the United States, China, and Vietnam (*Betanews* 2009). As of December 2006, CJ Internet, one of the subsidiaries of the largest multimedia conglomerate in Asia (CJ Group), also expanded into the publishing business with 329 employees (CJ Internet 2009). In the same year, another large media group, Onmedia, released its plan to join the online game industry, as it wished to leverage the existence of its game channel Ongamenet in the marketplace (Oh 2007). As of December 2009, the CJ group had acquired OnMedia for $367 million as part of its corporate strategy to expand in the cable market. As discussed in chapter 4, OnMedia has one of the two major cable game channels; therefore, with this deal completed, it is recorded as the most significant convergence between a game publisher and an online game channel (*Chosun Ilbo* 2009; Yang 2009).

These telecommunications and media corporations have been actively involved in the realms of new media technology and culture, because they believe content, including film and online gaming, is the key in the midst of the convergence of old and new media. In order to become a leader, or, at least to survive in the media and telecommunication markets, they are rapidly increasing their investment into the newly emerging online game sector. The convergence of telecommunications and broadcasting has been sought by many corporations, and online game industries are crucial parts of this trend, because online gaming is a mixture of content, broadcasting (eSports), and telecommunications. Only two years after its initial involvement in the online game sector, SK Telecom, the largest mobile service provider in Korea, announced that the company is not a telecommunications company but a global new media group, including game firms and mobile game portal GXG (Back 2005). SK Telecom has several game-related sectors, including IHQ (entertainment corporation), Ntreev Soft (online game developer), SK Telecom T1 (online game team), and SK Broadband. SK Telecom is also seeking cable channels. Through media convergence between telecommunications, broadcasting, and computers, SK Telecom has rapidly changed its corporate image from a mobile telecommunications company to a new media and content-driven media group.

Due to the surge of capital flow from many parties, from small venture capitals to big telecommunication and media corporations, domestic capital in the online game industry has dramatically increased over the last several years. As Aphra Kerr points out (2006b, 51), many countries have consolidated the game industry by partnering with big publishers in order to compete with Sony, Nintendo, and Microsoft in their game markets. However, concentration of ownership in Korea presents a much different situation. Some Korean venture capitalists consider online games as one of the most important new media technologies for bolstering the digital economy. Most of all, several sectors, including both media (CJ Internet and Onmedia) and telecommunications (KT and SK Telecom), consider online games as a necessary industry in which to have a presence. This convergence between media and online games as well as telecommunications and online games has expedited the concentration of the industry in terms of market share and ownership in the hands of a few leading game corporations.

It was not too long ago that game development was often characterized as the ultimate cottage industry for the information age (*The Economist* 1997, 175), but this statement has been losing its accuracy due to the increasing concentration of the online game industry in the hands of a few large corporations. As noted, the Korean online game industry is still a form of the cottage industry; however, fewer than 20 major corporations have swiftly expanded their scopes to become among the largest cultural corporations in the nation. Of course, as discussed in chapter 8, several domestic game corporations also welcome foreign game companies, while others establish joint ventures with foreign capital to secure constant capital flow and markets.

Historical Factors in the Growth of the Online Game Industry

There are several significant sociocultural and economic factors that have contributed to the rapid growth of the online game industry. Korean developers and publishers have been able to outperform major competitors, such as EA, Blizzard Entertainment, Nintendo, and Sony, due to the growth of IT, the subsequent distribution of nationwide high-speed networks, and thriving *PC bangs*. The swift development of IT and related policies has provided the foundation for the growth of online games. Korea has become the most wired nation in the world, with one of the highest rates of PC penetration. Moreover, as of December 2008, about 95% of Korean households were connected to broadband services, which is the highest percentage in the world (Strategy Analytics 2009). Against this backdrop, a survey conducted in 2006 showed that 66.6% of Korean respondents enjoyed online games, while about 25.4% of urban youth chose video games as the medium they most enjoyed in 2005 (Korea Game Industry Agency 2008; Cao and Downing 2008). This figure even increased to 74.9% in 2007. The majority of people still enjoyed watching televisions and movies; however, playing games became the third most popular activity during their free time (Ryu 2008). This acceptance into mainstream popular culture is evident in many ways, such as the success of games like *StarCraft*, *Lineage [I]* and *II*, and *AION*, the existence of celebrity professional gamers, and the organized league play of PC games, where tournaments are often broadcast on cable television (Kline, Dyer-Witheford, and de Peuter 2003).

In addition to the rapid growth of IT sectors, several historical events, such as Japan's colonial legacy in Korea and the Korean economic crisis in 1997 (discussed in chapter 2) have influenced the swift growth of the domestic online game industry. Because of Korea's colonization by Japan in the early twentieth century, as well as its concern about a Japanese cultural invasion, console games were never officially marketed in Korean on a mass scale (Chan 2008, 188), which has resulted in the growth of the online game sector.

As noted, console games are the most popular sector of the global game market; however, unlike in many other countries, online games are far more popular in Korea than the console variety, because the country had little exposure to console games, particularly because the majority of them were developed in Japan. Up until 1998, the Korean government banned Japanese cultural products, which included console games, film, and music due to the Japanese colonial legacy. With the ban lifted, Korea gradually opened the market to Japanese culture, with console games from the country making their appearance in the Korean market by 2002 (Chan 2008). Japanese companies that anticipated generating huge profits through gaining access to the Korean game market found the endeavor generated a negligible amount of revenue. Through its subsidiary company, Sony experienced a net loss in 2004 and 2005 when it began its sale of PlayStation 2. It subsequently delayed its launch of PlayStation 3 in Korea (Cho 2007a).

Sony finally began to sell its new PlayStation 3 in Korea in June 2007; however, it sold only 50,000 consoles through June 2008. Nintendo also sold only 40,000 consoles during the same period, while it sold 24.4 million consoles worldwide excluding Korea (Shim 2008). While Japanese console manufacturers (including Nintendo and Sony) experienced such difficulties in penetrating the Korean video game market, the Korean online game industry has been able to utilize the opportunity to develop its own online games.

It is interesting to note that the Korean game industry has utilized the economic downturn. It seems obvious that the economic recession is not hurting games, providing that when bad news hits, people seek escapist entertainment. Perhaps, it is no coincidence that the Korean online game industry took off about a decade ago, during the Asian financial crisis, the time the country's economy experienced the worst recession. As the recent growth of Korea's online game industries proves, Korea is clearly not the only country where computer gaming is becoming more popular amid the economic downturn, and Korean online game companies are intent on taking advantage of that (Kim 2009).

The State and the Game Industry in the Twenty-first Century

The Korean government put the online game industry in the center of policy as a major part of digital economy and culture. Since the early 1990s, the Korean government has wanted to develop communication businesses and information technologies to establish a high-tech industrial base, and the Korean government began to support the booming online game industry primarily with legal and financial forces, due to gaming's influence on young people, who are major consumers, as well as its relevance to youth culture. Korea, which was still a relatively underdeveloped country in the early 1980s, became one of the most vibrant and exceptional countries in terms of IT and later the online game industry, especially when compared to other countries. In the 1990s and the early twenty-first century, the Korean industry has experienced a dramatic transition to ICT-driven industrial structures, which include the online game industry. The Korean online game industry still has a traditional image as a cottage industry that employs fewer than 20 to 30 workers in most companies; however, a few large Korean corporations, including telecommunications, media, and electronics companies, as well as venture capital, have rapidly jumped into the business or expanded their investment in the game sector as one of their most important corporate investments. They have expanded their business areas into the online game industry, assuming the production and distribution of information and culture during the same period. They believed that the online game industry would become a lucrative business with the development of new communication technologies and increasing leisure time.

Against this backdrop, the Korean online game industry has been established due in part to the efforts of the government in supporting strong IT policy, which includes online gaming, in addition to fierce competition among local game companies. The influence of the Korean government on the online game industry spans innumerable institutions, from educational facilities to Internet access programs. Of most direct interest to game developers, however, is a patchwork of financial subsidies and legal incentives provided by the government to support the growth of high technology industry. Yet while the online game industry benefits from government financial support, it also collides with the regulatory face of government, as the rating of violent game content and speculative games embroils it in public controversy and political conflict, as is the case in many other countries (Dyer-Witheford and Sharman 2005, 187).

Given Korea's contributions to the creative industries, including game sectors, and its technological infrastructure, including broadband, it provides a great example of governmental strategies and industrial IT policies that have informed its movement into the century's participatory media such as Web 2.0 (Jenkins 2006; Hjorth and Chan 2009). Therefore, the government support was not meant to directly target the online game sector, but broadly the IT sector. As discussed in chapter 2, the rapid deployment of IT in Korea originated in 1995 when the government enacted the Framework Act on Information, which set up a comprehensive strategy for the KII (Ministry of Information and Communication 2004). This measure works as a conduit for the growth of the online game industry, because the swift developments of broadband services and PCs have facilitated online gaming and the industry.

As a more direct measure, over the last several years, the Korean government has provided legal support and financial subsidies to game developers, and it has increased its investment in a bid to nurture its software industry, with plans to continue. The online game industry, as opposed to other media such as film and television, had not been seen as central to the Korean government until the early twenty-first century. Although the government had nurtured IT, it had nothing to do with the emerging online game industry. Due to the rapid growth of the game industry driven by the market, the government acknowledged the importance of the game industry as a major business sector, as well as a mainstream cultural realm, particularly in relation to youth culture. As such, the direct influence of the Korean government has been as a policy maker as well as a financial supporter for the online game industry.

The Korean government first established the Integrated Game Support Center in 1999, which changed its name to the Korean Game Development and Promotion Institute in 2000, to develop the Korean game sector into a strategic export-oriented cultural industry. It has changed its name to the Korean Game Industry Agency in 2007 (Korean Game Industry Agency 2009).[1] As the government has supported the film industry with a plan to develop the cultural industry as a major part of the national economy, which has been driven by export, the government has also begun to support the online game industry for the national economy.

In 2004, the Korean government announced the "Long-term Promotion Plan of the Game Industry." According to the plan, the government was willing to support the game industry in becoming one of the three game-emperors in the world by increasing its market size to $10 billion by 2007, while increasing the number of employees in the game industry to 100,000 (Ham 2003). Although detailed plans were not articulated, it worked as a starting point for direct government support of the online game industry. Based on this plan, for example, in 2005 the Korean government announced a project to invest $20 million to support the development of graphics and virtual reality technologies in the games sector (Kim, M. H. 2005). As part of this plan, the government invested $13.5 million for the growth of the game industry and the creation of a game culture in 2006 (Ministry of Culture and Tourism 2006). Although the amount of this particular investment is small when compared with actual costs, it illustrates the intention of the Korean government to deliver on its promise of keeping to its policy (Jin and Chee 2009).

Meanwhile, the Korean government has also supported the game industry with its legal force. In April 2006, the government enacted the Relevant Implementation Order and Implementation Rules for the Game Industry Promotion Law (Promotion Law) to protect the game industry by differentiating it from speculative games, including poker games. The Promotion Law claims that "the game industry is the core industry of the next generation, which yields additional economic values"; therefore, the government wanted to develop an environment of growth for the game industry by providing legal support, such as tax breaks and copyrights. The online game industry is still a cottage industry, with fewer than 30 employees per company on average. When these companies cannot make revenues, the new tax-related law exempts 50% of corporate tax from game corporations for the next three years.

Finally, the liberalization of information and communication technologies, as one of the effects of the transnationalization of the online game industry, has been felt profoundly due to continuing foreign interest in large Korean game firms. Along with domestic-based firms, foreign-based TNCs have swiftly invested in the Korean online game industry with the objective of making profits while participating in the development of cutting-edge technologies. As a consequence of the liberalization of the market, foreign investors were holding around half of the shares at major Korean game firms such as NCsoft (41.8%) and NHN (51.4%) as of March 2007 (Cho 2007b). As detailed in chapter 8, several transnational game corporations have played a key role by establishing their subsidiaries or joint ventures in the Korean game market.

As such, the Korean government plays a proactive role in facilitating the further development of the domestic game industry. Instead of regulating and censoring the game industry, the government has liberalized the game market to foreigners, which has resulted in the rapid growth of foreign investment. The Korean online game industry and local creative industry has been strongly informed and supported by a strong government IT policy that insisted on high investment in IT infrastructure and offered funds to Internet service providers (Jin 2006). While the widespread availability of *PC bangs* played a key role in the distribution networks of online game companies in the domestic market in the first stage of the growth of online games, fierce competition among game developers and favorable government policies have played major roles in the continued growth of the game industry. In sum, government support for the online game industry is not an isolated effort but part of an ongoing government-initiated reform to build strong cultural industries, starting in the mid-1990s. The online game policies and regulations focusing on culture, technology, and economy have led to the formation of a prosperous new cultural industry on a global scale.

Summary

The Korean online game industry has witnessed phenomenal growth as it has become one of the core businesses of the new media sector, and game software has become representative of new media content for the twenty-first century. The Korean game industry has achieved one of the highest growth rates in the world, and the increasing number of game users and game firms has been dramatic. Korea, a small and underdeveloped country until the early 1980s, became a major power in today's world of digital technology, emerging as a cultural leader in pursuit of a new kind of empire (Yi 2006). Regardless of several competitors, such as China and the United States, the Korean online game industry has set global standards and led the global game industry, which has resulted in its status as the online game empire.

The development of its online game industry has not been without concerns, such as a phase of stagnation; market saturation; increasing competition, particularly with China; and structural imbalances. The apparent flourishing of online games is precarious to a certain extent after experiencing phenomenal growth over the last several years. The chief concern is that the online game industry is now in a phase of stagnation due to increasing competition. Several major online game companies, including NCsoft, have experienced eroding growth. For example, Webzen recorded a net loss of $55 million between 2005 and 2006 (Whang 2006). The profit of NCsoft also significantly decreased from $72 million in 2005 to $45.6 million in 2008, although the profits of the first quarter of 2009 was recorded at $43.4 million due to the success of *AION* (Kim and Kim 2009). Given that only a few games dominate the online game market, it is imperative to develop new games, which is more difficult because of severe competition and the difficulties in financing in the midst of the global economic recession.

In addition, Korean online game corporations have been confronted with a big challenge from China and other Asian countries. The Chinese online game industry may have had a late start, but it is growing faster than anywhere else. Several large Chinese companies, including Shanda, Netease.com, and Tencent, already enjoy a global presence, although it may be awhile before China overtakes Korea (Rhee and Wei 2009). The Korean game industry has been vibrant in the global market; however, it needs to develop its own unique strategy to compete against other global players, because the global market is becoming much more competitive.

In conclusion, the future of the Korean online game industry may depend on how two major issues are managed. On the one hand, the game industries have to deliberate on the ways in which they maintain and/or proliferate with the current boom of Korean online games against newly emerging online game firms in other Asian countries as well as Western countries. On the other hand, the Korean online game industry needs to develop new platforms by integrating the Internet-based online game with console games. Sony and Microsoft have been developing console-based online games since the early twenty-first century. Combinations of global game firms and local game companies, such as EA (United States) and Neowiz, THQ (United States) and Vertigo Games, and SCEI (Japan) and NCsoft, continue to work together to develop console-online platforms (Cho 2009). Currently, they are not significant in terms of market share; however, this clearly demonstrates that the market situation of the game industry will be more complicated and competitive, not only between online game firms but also between online and other platforms. In addition, Korean game firms must develop genres of online game software other than MMORPGs. Although they are currently dominant forms, one cannot predict the future of online gaming, so they need to develop diverse content.

To maintain its current status as an empire in online gaming, Korean policy makers and those in the game industries have to consider how to integrate the specificity of Korean online gaming into the logic of the global game market to create both diversity and commercial profits.

II
Game, Culture, and Digital Economy

4

eSports and Television Business in the Digital Economy

Introduction

The increasing popularity of online gaming and the live broadcasting of online game leagues on television channels and the Internet have expedited the growth of online games, particularly among mainstream Korean youth. eSports (electronic sport and the leagues that compete through networked games and related activities) saw its first league in 1998 when *StarCraft* became popular in Korea. With the growth of *PC bangs*, eSports has become one of the major activities among teens and those in their early twenties. Since then, several dozen online game leagues have grown in Korea, while a handful of major corporations, including Samsung and other telecommunications and media corporations, have invested in eSports as one of the new media and/or cultural businesses. Due to its commercial benefits, large corporations have begun to join the leagues, and several hundred registered professional gamers on twelve professional teams compete with each other for an annual $5 million in prize money; the number of game competitions for amateur gamers is increasing. Korea hosted the first World Cyber Games (WCG), dubbed the "Olympics of Computer Games," which were held in Seoul in 2001 and have been one of the most significant annual international eSports events.

The rapid growth of eSports is closely related to the media, particularly broadcasting. Primarily due to the existence of two cable television channels (Ongamenet and MBC Game), five Internet Protocol (IP) televisions, and two Web portals fully dedicated to game competitions, game players involved in professional gaming often become celebrities, supported by major corporate sponsorship and a loyal fan base as though they were television talents or movie stars. Unlike almost anywhere else in the world, Koreans who are good at playing digital games are highly regarded, which is one of the most intriguing things about Korea. The main medium for eSports coverage in most countries is the Internet; however, in Korea, eSports events are regularly televised by cable channels as well as later through IP televisions. Many people aspire to be like these famous professional gamers, and this contributes to the national passion for games. Koreans are internationally renowned for their enthusiastic game play, and most Korean gamers worry less about the negative "geek" taboo that gamers put up with in other parts of the world, as in North America. To the contrary, professional gamers in Korea are idolized, marrying supermodels and engaging in other celebrity activities that are deemed worthy of spectacle and intrigue by the general populace (Jin and Chee 2008).

Yet, at the same time, relatively little has been written about the nature of eSports, so the academic investigation of competitive computer gaming, also called eSports, is still in its infancy. This chapter examines the development of eSports—the intricate interrelationship among online gaming, media, and sport. It documents the history of eSports, and then it discusses the ways in which eSports became a cultural phenomenon in the Korean context. Second, it investigates the role of eSports in the growth of the online game industry and professional game players. Finally, it discusses the reasons that cable and network broadcasters are invested in eSports by focusing on the convergence of telecommunications and broadcasting, which is one of the major issues of the digital economy and culture.

Convergence of Culture and Digital Economy

Understanding eSports is complex because it involves several different cultural and economic phenomena. eSports is difficult to categorize as a cultural genre or sporting event because eSports is a new area developed through the convergence of culture and technology, culture and sport, and culture and business. As online gaming has merged with IT, which is essential for the growth of the online game industry, eSports has become a key domain in the digital economy. In fact, eSports has several meanings, and it is important to understand eSports as the convergence of the electronic games, sports, and media. eSports is not only the convergence of sport and media, but of online gaming, sport, and media. Unlike other professional sports emphasizing the sport–business–television nexus (Rowe 1996), eSports has shown its unique convergence of the content–sport–television business nexus. Therefore, unlike the integration between sport and media in many sports having professional divisions, such as in basketball and baseball, eSports should be understood as a more complex process.

eSports is an exemplary case of digital convergence, which entails the fusion of a combination of technologies to allow more services and/or products to become available to consumers via a wider range of digital devices, including cable television, IP television, and the Internet (Baldwin et al. 1996, 3–4). Baldwin and others (1996) view media convergence from three perspectives: consolidation through industry alliances and mergers; the combination of technology and network platforms; and the integration between services and markets. Henry Jenkins (2006, 2–3) further details the fusion of technology, industry, culture, and society. He argues that media convergence can be categorized into three major areas: the flow of content across multiple media platforms; the cooperation between multiple media industries; and the migratory behavior of media audiences, who will go almost anywhere in search of the kinds of entertainment experiences they want.

Although developments in a wide-range of industries have traditionally exerted a certain degree of influence on the computer and video game industries, recent advances have led toward a much greater fusion of gaming-related content, markets, and technologies. Furthermore, although the concept of convergence is certainly not new, the complexities associated with it make it difficult to ascertain a precise conceptual framework, especially one that is relevant to the dynamic nature of the games industry (Ip 2008, 200). The convergence of online games with digital media has, of course, two levels of integration: the first is the integration between electronic gaming and sport and the second is between electronic gaming and digital media, which is convergence between culture and business. The importance of the convergence between electronic gaming and sport, as the term eSports signifies, needs to be discussed; however, this chapter focuses on the nature of the convergence of culture and business due to the importance of eSports as a primary part of the digital economy. These concepts are not mutually exclusive due to the close relationship between media structure and content. Convergence is not possible without the integration of popular culture and digital media, which is a platform of the ground of playing their culture (Jin 2009).

To begin with, there are some avenues that offer useful starting points for understanding the convergence of online gaming and sport. There have been several previous studies that emphasize the interrelation of sport and media, including the escalating commercialization and mediatization of the Olympics, the World Cup soccer game, and the World Series baseball game (Rowe 2004, 1996). One of the most useful theories scrutinizing the social and cultural interface between the media and sport is David Rowe's (2004) notion of media sports cultural complex. David Rowe (2004, 1996) bridges historical understanding, the structural influence of market forces, the role of cultural discourse, and myths in the production and consumption of sport. However, Rowe does not discuss the relationship between online gaming and sport. As a reflection of their recent development, video games (particularly online games) are hardly mentioned in these accounts. When previous studies bridged sport and media, as in the case of the Olympic Games, soccer, ice hockey, and American football, they did not give much attention to the convergence among sports, electronic games, and media. Because scholars define the concept of eSports based on sport, it is not surprising to see the importance of sport in these studies.

In fact, there are several interesting interpretations of eSports as part of sports. Oxford defines eSports as "a computer game played in professional competitions, especially when it is watched by fans and broadcast on the Internet or on television." Michael Wagner (2006) defines eSports as "an area of sport activities that includes sport activities in which people develop and train mental or physical abilities in the use of information and communication technologies." As such, these definitions focus more on the nature of electronic sport based on the basic idea of sport. However, even when we admit the importance of sport in eSports, it is only a limited interpretation. eSports, which has a short history, already expanded its concept to relevant activities beyond competition and broadcasting.

Only a decade ago, online gaming was not a major part of sports or culture. In addition, the online game sector was not a tangible business entity because it had been considered a cottage industry, which had fewer than 20 employees in each company. Online games were primarily an entertainment product that people found fun. The issue of pleasure has been a niggling thorn in the side of the business (Kline, Dyer-Witheford, and de Peuter 2003). However, eSports has made itself one of the most significant of the cultural industries in recent years. Online gaming is not for fun but for business—one of the most profitable businesses in fact, because it is a great combination of electronic games, culture, and media that young people pursue. The rise of online gaming is proof that the $32 billion a year video game industry has come of age as a business as well as a sport (Goodale 2008).

eSports is a gaming, computing, media, and sports event all at once, and online game competitions, including the WCG, highlight a shift whereby the relationship between media and sport is no longer one of structural interrelation—respective industries and end-users serving the others' needs in terms of content, audiences, and profits—but of material integration (Hutchins 2008, 852). eSports represents a logical yet radical extension of this process, integrating the organizational, physical, and technological basis of competition. This arrangement has been made possible by the IT revolution and rapid expansion in the availability, capability, and popularity of interactive digital communications technologies (Hutchins 2008, 852). Sports are enabled through communications and media systems, which constitute the symbolic and physical environment of game production, consumption, and distribution (Kline, Dyer-Witheford, and de Peuter 2003). In Korea, when eSports started (in 2000), about 21.4% of Internet users were using computers for online games; in 2006, that percentage increased to 55.5%. In addition, the total number of Internet users rapidly increased from 19 million in 2000 to 34 million in 2006 (Ministry of Information and Communication 2006).

More importantly, convergence in eSports happens as part of the digital economy. Several big corporations, including those dealing with media and telecommunications such as Samsung, have acquired and/or created their own online game teams. In particular, several leading telecommunications corporations in Korea have rapidly initiated corporate convergence among online game teams, media (cable or IP television), and telecommunications systems, which is convergence between not only sport and media but also media and telecommunications. These corporations certainly understand changing cultural phenomena among young people, and they plan to utilize the convergence between culture and media as a new business strategy to exploit synergy effects. As Dan Schiller (2000, 130) points out, "the advertising community had already begun to fix on one of a handful of 'old-standby' program genres with a demonstrated global popularity: sports and games, in a plethora of formats and business models. Games in turn engaged the potential implicit in the first of cyberspace's critical typifying features: its interactivity." Because young people who enjoy and watch online game competitions are major customers of the corporations' mobile technologies, they want to have online game teams and cable and/or IP television channels in order to maximize their profits. As Henry Jenkins (2006) points out, digital media institutions, including broadcasting and telecommunications companies, have acknowledged the migratory behavior of young people, and they have had to follow their lead to change their focus to online game businesses. Television had taken over sport, and television this time has taken over online gaming. eSports, which is a mix of online gaming, media, and sport, therefore, should be understood as a mass market commercial product, developed and distributed by established media corporations as well as new media as a primary part of the digital economy.

Historical Development of eSports

eSports has been an important subsidiary element that has helped increase the mainstream saturation of online game players. The popularity of eSports works to merge different social interest groups, industry players, and online game consumers (Chung 2008, 313). The growth of eSports and the development and popularity of professional online gamers, which is discussed in chapter 5, are closely related to each other in this new area. eSports has facilitated and expedited the growth of online games and professional online game culture, which has made professional gamers a major part of the daily lives of Korean youth.

Video games have been played competitively since their inception, and the origin of eSports began with arcade games.[1] In particular, Twin

Galaxies, founded in 1981, which keeps track of high scores on many classic arcade games, including pinball statistics, played a key role in the development of eSports. Twin Galaxies' role as a scorekeeper grew in importance as player rankings became a major focus of the media. As the pioneer in ranking the top players, Twin Galaxies was called upon to bring the superstar players together for many well-publicized contests and media events. As Twin Galaxies continued to rank top players, the first national video game team was formed to represent the United States, made up of a select cadre of the best talent. The U.S. National Video Game Team, with Walter Day as the founding team captain, issued international video game challenges to Japan, the United Kingdom, and Italy, even hand-delivering proclamations to their respective embassies in Washington, D.C. Eventually, the team toured the United States, Europe, and Asia during the 1980s (Twin Galaxies 2004).

However, this early stage of competition was not the same as the current game competition, because the games were not televised, and eSports matches were not broadcast over the Internet. As Brett Hutchins (2008) points out, eSports is a gaming, computing, media, and sports event all at once—familiar in its presentation format but unfamiliar in its content. Twin Galaxies acted as the organizer and record keeper of game competitions instead of participating in the game as a team.

The first regularly televised eSports program was the Australian game show *A*mazing*, which would show two children competing in various Nintendo games in order to win points. *A*mazing* aired between 1993 and 1998 on the Seven Network, and the show pitted teams from two primary schools against each other during the course of a week. Points gained by each contestant during the week were totaled up to decide the winning school at the end of each week (IMDB 1994). Teams consisted of two players, who would take part in spelling challenges before venturing into one of two mazes to hunt for letters which made up the word they had just figured out. The letters were hidden among many obstacles and confusing paths. Toward the end of the show, there was a deciding match of *Super Mario Kart* to see which team played the final round. The finale consisted of keys instead of letters, inside the maze. The more keys the players found, the more points their school got (Ieon 2007).

Development of eSports in Korea

Although Australia first started eSports with Nintendo games, eSports in the field of online gaming started its first league in 1997 when *StarCraft* became popular in Korea. eSports was originally used as a narrow definition of electronic sport leagues that competed through network games in Korea; however, with the growth of online games, eSports now includes not only competition through network games but also the cultural and industrial activities related to network games (Korea Game Industry Agency 2006). In Korea, eSports became one of the most popular activities among teens and those in their early twenties with the growth of *PC bangs*. People enjoyed online games before the growth of *PC bangs*; however, the rapid growth of *PC bangs* and high-speed Internet contributed to the growth of online gaming. The *StarCraft* obsession evolved from being the game of choice in *PC bangs* in scattered tournaments in the late 1990s. At that time, the youth wanted to enjoy online games with other players, and they began to engage in online gaming through Battle.Net, an online gaming service provided by Blizzard Entertainment in the United States. Spotting the audience potential, promoters soon formed professional leagues (Wallace 2007). In December 1997, *PC bang* chains opened the first national online game league, known as Korea Pro Gamers League. The development of this early form of eSports was made possible by the IT revolution and rapid expansion in the availability, capabilities, and popularity of interactive digital communications technologies, which Korea played a large role in developing (Hutchins 2008). eSports, as a cultural and economic phenomenon, became one of the most popular activities among teens and those in their twenties in Korea.

eSports grew with the live broadcasting of competitions on cable television networks, which expedited the growth of online games, particularly among young Koreans. As in many other countries, the dot-com boom between 1991 and 2000 accelerated the growth of eSports in Korea, because the Korean government drove the growth with financial and legal support in the midst of the growth of IT. The Ministry of Culture and Tourism supported eSports by organizing different social groups in order to promote positive public awareness of online game play (Chung 2008). In Korea, the term eSports was originally presented by Ji-Won Park, Minister of the Department of Culture and Tourism, in

February 2000, when he used the term at the inaugural meeting of the Korea e-Sports Association (formerly the 21st Century Pro-Game Association). It has been an official term indicating online game competitions and related activities, including professional game teams, broadcasting, and fan community activities ever since (Samsung Economic Research Institute 2005a). The market size of Korean eSports has exponentially increased. Including broadcasting, eSports leagues, and corporate sponsorship, the eSports market increased from $26.7 million in 2004 to $39.5 million in 2005 (a 48% increase); it was expected to increase 28.8% annually to $77.4 million in 2007 and to $120.7 million in 2010 (Samsung Economic Research Institute 2005a). Although this figure is still far smaller than other professional sports (e.g., the market size of professional baseball was $160 million in 2005), eSports certainly shows potential to be one of the major sports event in the near future due to the rapid growth of game users and fans (Lee, T. 2006).

With the rapid growth of online games, the Korean government has overhauled legislation in a bid to nurture the software industry, including online games. In the games and content sector, for example, the government planned to invest $20 million to support the development of graphics and virtual reality technologies toward the goal of placing five local firms on the U.S. NASDAQ market by 2010 (Kim 2007). As part of this plan, in 2010 the Korean government is investing $13.6 million in the game sector (Choi 2010). The government also announced its Game Industry Promotion 5-Year Plan in 2004 in order to develop eSports and the online game industry. This plan included academic research to support, diverse policy development, eSports culture festivals, and eSports-only online game development (Ministry of Culture and Tourism 2006). The professional gamers also have tax deduction benefits for their monetary awards. The tax on their game awards is only 3.3%, compared to 22% for other awards (Korea e-Sports Association 2008b). The job opportunities opened up with the expansion of the cultural sector resonate with the Korean government as it tried to reach nearly full employment as a means of remaining in office, and of endorsing a mode of citizenship through employment. Culture and work are critical to policy and thus to change. Since the late 1990s, work has been a site of endless government activity (McRobbie 2002). Partly due to favorable government policies and social infrastructure, online games have made significant leaps in popularity. In fact, the activities of cyberathletes signal the advent of a qualitatively distinct phenomenon, and this term has been coined and entered into popular usage because competitive organized gaming represents both continuity and marked discontinuity with the established relationship between broadcast media and sports (Hutchins 2008, 857).

In 2000, when the Korean government started its support for the growth of eSports, three game leagues, including Korea Pro Gamers League, Progamer Korea Open, and Korea Pro Game League, gained recognition as official online game competitions. The three major leagues also facilitated the birth and rise of approximately 40 online game teams (Korea Game Industry Agency 2007a). However, the burst of the dot-com bubble and the lack of linkage with broadcasting corporations caused the rapid decline of these leagues, and many online game teams shut down and/or sold their teams to other corporations (see chapter 6). Nevertheless, the first online game showed up on television under the name of *PKO* at Tooniverse in 1999, and the owner of Onmedia, which is the largest cable network in Korea, opened a game specialty cable channel, Ongamenet, in the same year (Korea Game Industry Agency 2006, 488). In the mid-1990s and early twenty-first century, Korean policy makers had deregulated advanced telecommunications and broadcasting applications, causing the rapid growth of the Korean broadband infrastructure. The vast broadband infrastructure in Korean furthermore favored the creation of television stations that were able to focus on broadcasting computer gaming events. The combination of these elements resulted in a gaming culture in which individual *StarCraft* players were able to gain cultlike followings similar to professional athletes and movie stars (Wagner 2006).

Growth of World Cyber Games
As a reflection of its emerging market and its convergence with youth culture, Korea initiated the first-ever international game competition, and the WCG—now one of the major international online game competitions—emerged from a vibrant Korean gaming culture. The eSports culture is a Korean attempt to connect Korea to the world through global media consumption of online games (Chung 2008). The first event was held in Seoul in 2001, attracting more than 430 competitors from 37

countries (during the WCG period, approximately 389,000 competed for the Grand Finals) for $300,000 in prize money for those who advanced to the Grand Finals, in addition to another $300,000 for the league (table 4.1). Each subsequent year has seen the event grow, and, while the event was hosted in Korea until 2003, it has been held in several major cities around the world since then, including San Francisco (United States) in 2004, Singapore in 2005, Monza (Italy) in 2006, Seattle (United States) in 2007, and Cologne (Germany) in 2008. When Cologne hosted the WCG, the participants numbered as many as 800 from 78 countries, and the total prize for the Grand Finals soared to $470,000 (World Cyber Games 2008).

Because contestants must progress through preliminary rounds in their own countries in order to qualify for the WCG Grand Finals, organizers claimed that more than 1 million gamers worldwide entered the national preliminary rounds (Games Press 2008). Coverage of the event was available via the WCG television Web site, and selected reports appeared in media outlets internationally, including BBC News and CNN International (Hutchins 2008). Games played cover different genres, including FPS (*Counter-Strike*), sports (*FIFA Soccer*), and real-timer strategy (*StarCraft*); Korea has led the competition with an overall 16 gold medals cumulative from 2001, followed by Germany (10) and the United States (10) (World Cyber Games 2008). Gaming is conducted through networked computers, which are designed to communicate beyond national boundaries via the Internet. While the WCG takes place in a single location using a local area network, the games played, such as *Counter-Strike* and *Warcraft*, are played competitively and informally by, and between, tens of thousands of gamers situated around the globe on a daily basis (Hutchins 2008, 862). Sport leagues held in Korea and by the WCG have many different characteristics. Korean eSports has progressed beyond a cultural phenomenon among youth and has become one of the major digital businesses in Korea. With hundreds of thousands of viewers and fans, more than ten media-broadcasted online game competitions, and many large corporate sponsors, online gaming has become one of the most popular cultural and business entities in Korea, while the WCG operates on a much smaller scale and is seen as a festival for game maniacs around the world. The success of WCG has created subsequent eSports games, including the World eSports Games in 2005

Table 4.1
History of the World Cyber Games Finals

	2001	2002	2003	2004	2005	2006	2007	2008
Countries	37	45	55	63	70	70	75	78
Participants	430	462	562	642	800	700	700	800
Total Prize	300	300	350	420	435	462	448	470
Host Location	Seoul, Korea	Daejon, Korea	Seoul, Korea	San Francisco, United States	Singapore, Singapore	Monza, Italy	Seattle, United States	Cologne, Germany

Note: Monetary awards are given in U.S. dollars ($1,000).
Source: Data from World Cyber Games 2009.

and World e-Sports Masters in 2006. eSports has rapidly become one of the major global events primarily due to its popularity among young people who are increasingly enjoying online games, and it is one of the major cultural activities for youth in Korea.

eSports and Broadcasting Business

As the sports media have proven to be of phenomenal appeal to the global audience, eSports has rapidly become one of the major television events among young people. Within the public domain, young people are perceived to be especially influenced by the powerful effects of media messages, with widely expressed concern focused on their inability to be discerning readers of the sporting texts, and to their susceptibility to imitate the inappropriate on-and off-field exploits of their favorite game stars (Lines 2000). Unlike other professional sports and their close relation to media, eSports has its own unique characteristics, as the name implies. It has been named a sport because the game's result is decided through competition, as in sports, but the competition is between people through a network. In order to be eSports, a game has to meet certain criteria: (1) the game must be between people, instead of between people and computers, (2) the result should be decided within a limited time due to broadcasting issues; therefore, several neverending MMORPG games such as *Lineage [I]*, *II*, and *World of Warcraft* cannot be part of competitions for the broadcasting business, (3) cooperation between both physical and mental abilities—therefore, several games, including poker and Go (Baduk: a strategic board game for two people), which do not need physical activities, are eliminated, and (4) the decision should be decided according to real abilities instead of fortune; therefore, gambling games such as poker and go-stop (Korean version of a poker game) should not be part of eSports (Samsung Economic Research Institute 2005a).

The media, particularly broadcasting, has played a major role in the growth of eSports in Korea, because media create audiences, which are necessary for eSports. Although there have been many professional and amateur online game players, the popularity of online gaming cannot be guaranteed without broadcasting. Unlike other major professional sports events where network broadcasters play a key role, cable and

IP televisions have taken the major role in the growth of eSports. In Korea, it did not take too much time to reach more than 1 million viewers per game on cable television. In 2004, one online game had 100,000 views, and, in 2004, the SKY Pro League final attracted as many as 120,000 spectators to an outdoor stadium in the southern city of Busan. Due to the rapid growth of eSports, existing sports have experienced recession. For example, when 120,000 people watched the online game in Busan, there were only 30,000 people attending the baseball all-star game held on the same day on July 17, 2004. Every sport has its star players, such as Michael Jordan or Tiger Woods, and eSports is no different; however, eSports may need a superstar just to let the world know it exists (Goodale 2008).

As for the dedication of broadcasting to the growth of eSports, two key cable networks have two major game leagues: MBC Game's Star League and Ongamenet's Pro League. MBC Game airs Star League games for 5 days, from Saturday to Wednesday. When the league starts, each team has four individual games and one team game (two gamers each) per week, and when one team wins three games, it becomes the winner of the week and moves on to the next round. There are two different competitions, and there are a total of ten games per week. Meanwhile, Ongamenet has its Ongamenet Pro League on Thursdays and Fridays every week. In the final stage, Ongamenet Pro League has the first and second teams compete with each other in the championship game. Star League winners get $40,000, and Pro League winners get $80,000. In addition, the reward of the championship game at the Pro League is $50,000. Games have been televised for seven years by the two cable channels, and they have loyal fans. Ongamenet, the largest game channel, reaches 3 to 4 million viewers during the 6-to-10 p.m. primetime window, and its competitor, MBC Game, draws 1.5 million viewers at the same time for its own leagues (Wallace 2007). Several million viewers watch these events over the Internet and on television, captivated by seeing what professional gamers can do.

The two cable channels, Ongamenet and MBC Game, are leaders in eSports. Ongamenet is a subsidiary cable company of OnMedia, which is the largest cable and satellite broadcaster in Korea. Ongamenet was the first online game specialty channel in the world, and it started 24-hour game programs in June 2001. As of January 2005, it broadcasts to 10 million cable subscribers, and about 2.5 million subscribers enjoy live game shows and/or video-on-demand services (Ongamenet 2008). Ongamenet opened the world's first eSports dedicated stadium with 500 seats for regular eSports tournaments. Ongamenet hosts two major eSports leagues and airs more than 40 eSports leagues, including local game leagues. As a reflection of the popularity of online gaming, Ongamenet has been one of the most popular channels (among 87 cable channels in Korea), especially for the 13- to 25-year-old male demographic (Samsung Economic Research Institute 2005b). MBC Game is a subsidiary cable channel of MBC Plus and also began its 24-hour game broadcasting in 2001.

In 2007, the Korea e-Sport Association recreated a new team league known as ShinHan Bank Proleague, formally known as SKY Pro League. Unlike MBC Star League and Ongamenet Pro League, the ShinHan Bank Proleague has been televised on both cable channels at the same time. ShinHan Bank, as an official supporter of the league, pays $5 million per year (Korea e-Sports Association 2008c). As commercial media distribution channels were expanded nationally, online game sponsorship expenditures soared (Schiller 2000). Besides the two cable channels, two Internet televisions (Gom TV and Pandora TV), two Internet portals (Daum and Naver), and one IP television (Hana TV) broadcast ShinHan Bank Proleague live (Korea e-Sports Association 2008c). Considering their convergence of telecommunications and broadcasting, these broadcasters have come to play a major part in the production of professional game leagues.

As such, eSports has been popular, and, as of November 2007, there were 21 online games in five different game genres in which professional gamers competed. They consisted of real-time strategy simulation games (*StarCraft* and *WarCraft III*), FPS games (*Sudden Attack* and *A.V.A.*), sports (*FIFA* and *Shot Online*), racing (*KartRider* and *City Racer*), and others. Due to the increasing popularity of online gaming, and particularly thanks to the growth of eSports (mainly through cable and Internet television channels), the total number of online game competitions and the total amount of reward money has rapidly increased. In 1999, there were 72 games and $1.5 million was awarded (table 4.2); in 2005, there were 278 games that generated prizes in the amount of $5 million, the highest thus far (Korea e-Sports Association 2008b; Korea Game Indus-

Table 4.2
Domestic eSports Competitions

	1999	2000	2001	2002	2003	2004	2005	2006	2007
Number of Competitions	72	82	93	187	144	98	278	124	70
Money Award	1.5	2.0	3.0	3.5	4.0	4.5	5.0	3.3	1.8

Note: Monetary awards are given in U.S. dollars ($1 million).
Source: Data from Korea e-Sports Association 2008c.

try Agency 2006, 495). Ongamenet started its satellite broadcasting of online game competitions in October 2006. The cable channel has also aired the WCG, which is the largest game competition. As discussed in chapter 6, professional gamers must digest these heavy schedules and games; they have suffered from overload with virtually no holidays.

Business Models of eSports in Broadcasting

There are several significant business models for eSports, including advertising, sponsorship, and exclusive broadcasting rights. The major business model of broadcasters in eSports has, however, shifted in many ways. Most of all, the exclusive broadcasting rights have changed. Unlike other sports, including basketball and soccer, in which broadcasters pay transit share to the sports league, eSports broadcasters receive transit share from the league or individual games (Korea Game Industry Agency 2007a, 508). The two cable broadcasters secured consistent revenue sources through this unique business model until recent years. The Korea e-Sports Association has shifted the model by selecting a major sports league model since 2007. Now the two cable broadcasters must pay transit share to the International eSport Group (IEG), which is a contractor of the Korea e-Sports Association. The two cable broadcasters have to produce game shows through sponsorship as well as advertising. The Korea e-Sports Association has changed the business model to secure stable revenues for the association and eSports.

For broadcasters, both cable and new media, advertising has been a major part of their revenues. In 2007, the two cable channels (Ongamenet and MBC Game) earned $203 million through advertising, while new media (IP televisions) secured $4.3 million (Korea e-Sports Association 2008b). Because OnMedia, the mother company of Ongamenet, used to earn revenues mainly through advertising (63%), it is not surprising to know that Ongamenet also secures a certain amount of revenue from advertising. Another major revenue source is subscription fees, which contributes about 29%, and further sources include marketing events. Unlike other sports events and/or cultural events, there are no admission fees to enter the game studio. Because the admission to game studios is open to the public, their revenue structure is still limited.

Corporate sponsors from several electronics and telecommunications giants—such as Samsung Electronics, SK Telecom, and Korea Telecom Freetel (KTF), which merged with Korea Telecom (KT) in 2009—as well as media companies and financial sectors have become critical for the development of eSports and professional gamers. For example, the ShinHan Bank Proleague is built upon a business model that contains a single large sponsor. ShinHan Bank is counting on unbridled gamer passion, which it hopes extends to the tens of millions of fans who play eSports for fun. Samsung Electronics has funded the WCG since 2001. This sponsorship highlights Korea's centrality to the shape and structure of the culture and business of eSports, both nationally and globally, with the strength of Korea's gaming culture combined with a major manufacturer of digital technologies (Hutchins 2008). Of course, these corporate sponsors identify the potential value of eSports. The WCG is sold to investors as a cybergames festival that also serves as a trading event for multinational ICT and gaming companies and investment capital, with a game business conference and an exhibition included in its schedule. This serves as a forum and market driver for the consolidation of eSports as a unique technological phenomenon (Hutchins 2008). Due to the success of the two cable channels with the growth of eSports, several television channels, and other new media, particularly Internet television, have invested and expanded their business in the eSports area.

Business Models in New Media

Cable television is not the only media sector seeking to turn eSports into television programming these days. As of January 2009, there were 11 broadcasters, including a network broadcaster, two cable channels, five

Internet televisions, two Internet portals, and one satellite television station regularly broadcasting eSports leagues. In 2006, there were only four television channels broadcasting eSports events, but the number of broadcasters and their involvement rapidly increased. In recent years, five Internet televisions, including Gom TV, Pandora TV, Africa TV, Hana TV, and Mega TV, have begun to air online game competitions. One satellite television, TV Media, also airs eSports leagues (Korea Game Industry Agency 2008b). Among these, IP television channels have rapidly increased their subscribers and competed with cable television channels. For example, Hana TV, started in September 2006, has already secured 540,000 subscribers. Because the number of subscribers will be more than 3.5 million in 2010, and IP television will be one of the major media forms in the digital era, several more IP televisions will join the eSports market in the near future and act as a medium for the growth of eSports in the Korean context.

IP television is a new digital medium resulting from the convergence of telecommunications and broadcasting. Several major telecommunications corporations, including KT and Hanaro Telecom, had already started their services in 2008, and SK Broadband and LG Dacom began their services in January 2009. Several of these telecommunications corporations own online game teams, and they plan to provide several entertainment programs, including online game competitions. For example, KT has converged with KTF, which owned KTF MagicNs (online game team), and SK Broadband, which is a subsidiary company of SK Telecom, which owns SK Telecom T1 (online game team), plan to utilize IP television for the exposure of their online game teams, and the revenues of their corporations (Lee 2008). Telecommunications companies have utilized strategically advantageous positions in the online game business, because consumers pay monthly subscription fees and online service charges to a telecom operator (Kerr 2006b, 56). By nature, telecommunication companies have converged in several areas, including cable, IP television, Web portal, and game teams. Telecommunications corporations have rapidly jumped into the eSports business, both in terms of broadcasting and creating/owning game teams, because eSports has become popular among young people who are major customers for them. Telecommunications corporations have become larger and presumably more powerful in the eSports area.

The country's two largest Web portals, Naver and Daum, have also launched an Internet protocol television service since 2008. Naver, the largest Web portal, first launched IP television in collaboration with the leading broadband firm KT. Daum, the second-largest Web portal and search engine company, announced that it will team up with U.S.-based Microsoft Corporation and Celrun Co. to enter the IP television market. These corporations believe that IP television, a television service delivered through a high-speed Internet network, will generate new revenue sources with interactive services such as advertising and e-commerce. In particular, Naver plans to provide its popular online game services and other services through IP television in an effort to expand its customer base (Jin, H. J. 2008a). In fact, these cable, satellite, IP television, and Web portal outlets believe that they are able to secure new revenue sources through subscription fees, advertisements, and corporate support, while producing new content which predominantly involves online game culture. The increase in popularity of eSports also creates new job categories, including professional game players, game casters, game commentators, and observers who catch interesting moments to show to the television viewers, comparable to cameramen in sports broadcasting.

Online game competitions are not popular on network channels, because eSports matches are not officially recognized as sports games. Currently, SBS, one of three major television network broadcasters in Korea, hosts and broadcasts *Game Show, Amusing World*, on Fridays (60 minutes), as a reflection of the popularity of online games in cable and Internet media (2008). Although it is a game show televised once a week, unlike other eSports leagues on cable television channels, the show has contributed to expanding the range of viewers, not only to young game fanatics but also to a more general audience. In particular, SBS, as a commercial broadcaster, plans to develop eSports as a new television genre (SBS 2008). However, network broadcasters cannot broadcast online game leagues because the current broadcasting law prohibits indirect advertisement. For example, because professional gamers wear their uniforms indicating corporate sponsors, for instance NASCAR, the network broadcasters are not able to air the games.

As such, for commercial broadcasters, and in particular cable companies, eSports emerges as a highly desirable business for several reasons. First, it attracts large and passionately devoted audiences who are primarily 18 to 34 years old. Because they are significant consumers for many advertisers, including for telecommunications, electronics, and media corporations, commercial broadcasters are able to secure lucrative advertising revenues (Park, H. 2006). Second, eSports is much cheaper than many quality dramas in terms of production cost. In order to produce one-hour-long quality dramas, broadcasters have had to pay $250,000 on average in recent years; however, online game competitions in studios are much cheaper. Third, eSports is associated with positive images of culture and new media. Broadcasters, including both cable and IP televisions, are keen about the emerging multimedia environment, and they believe that eSports is on the cutting edge for their business future. As participation in, and the hosting of, major sports competitions became a marker of national economic, technological, and political progress (Larson and Park 1993), hosting major eSports leagues becomes one of the most significant economic, cultural, and technological activities in digital society.

The broadcasting business of eSports expanded, for example, from $15.8 million in 2004 to $19.3 million in 2005 (a 22% increase; Samsung Economic Research Institute 2005a) and has become a major battleground between media and telecommunications industries. Because both industries are rapidly expanding through convergence of the two sectors, the online game business will be one of the primary businesses in the midst of the growth of the digital era. In particular, telecommunications and broadcasting industries focus on IP television because they believe IP television should be a leading new media, dominating the new media sector due to its convergence of the Internet and telecommunications. According to one survey, in 2012, IP television will consist of 23% of the broadcasting market, only behind network broadcasters (Media Future Institute 2007). Among new media, IP television would also be the most influential medium, followed by DMB and WiBro; therefore, the increase in the number of IP televisions will greatly influence the growth of eSports in the future. These areas in particular are expected to grow primarily because eSports is a great example of the convergence of content, media, and sport, which young people are crazy about. It is crucial to understand eSports' economic traits due to its prominent role in Korea's digital economy.

Summary

eSports has stepped into a growth period, and the numbers of games and gamers has dramatically increased. Online games and eSports have been considered as one of the major youth cultures, which are enjoyed by half of Koreans. Digital games are defined based on specific combinations of technical, social, cultural, and economic characteristics and not on exclusive, essential ones (Jenkins 2002; Raessens 2005). Although eSports shares several characteristics with popular sport events, such as football, soccer, and baseball, it also has several unique connections to new media and information technologies. In order to enjoy online games as content, people need computers, networks, and display systems. In particular, the recent development of DMB and WiBro have facilitated the growth of eSports because people are able to enjoy online games through these wireless telecommunications technologies. Cyberathletic competition cannot be thought of in terms of media or sport or computer gaming. The institutional and material boundaries separating them have imploded, leading to the creation of a new social form, eSports (Hutchins 2008, 865). However, eSports should also be understood as a major part of digital economy due to its importance as a new business model converging culture and IT, which are two major areas for the growth of digital economy.

In Korea, eSports is not only for fun but also for culture and economy. Through the convergence of culture and technology, and later with the media business, eSports has become one of the most lucrative businesses, which has resulted in the rapid involvement of several industries, including the telecommunications, media, and electronics sectors. They have utilized the convergence of culture and business to attract young people, who are their major customers. They have noticed the migratory behavior of Korean youth, from traditional entertainment and cultural activities to a new cultural and cutting-edge technological area. Several mega media giants, including MBC, which is one of the three network broadcasters, and OnMedia, which is the largest cable company in Korea, have established special game channels. Several large corporations, including Samsung and CJ, as well as telecommunications companies, have expanded their investment to the online game sector by investing in cable or IP television businesses, while owning professional game teams, as discussed in chapter 5. Telecommunications and media corporations pursue convergence due in large part for the desire to maximize profits through the concentration of media companies, because vertical and horizontal integrations bring synergy effects (Chambers and Howard 2005; Chan-Olmsted 1998). For Korean telecommunications and media corporations, eSports has been a new business area that brings profit and an enhanced image to their companies, due to its cutting-edge commodity value. The convergence of culture, new technology, and sport with young people who are major customers is a must-have business.

In sum, eSports can be seen as a new application of a range of technological, cultural, and economic inventions, and as the convergence of these individual components. eSports business is expected to grow rapidly due to its importance as not only entertainment and culture but also due to its business-oriented industrial characteristics. eSports as an emerging digital culture and economy will be further developed because the online game area is expected to grow about 20% annually in the near future. Because of the rapid penetration of the Internet (80.6% of Koreans use the Internet as of December 2008, the highest percentage in the world) and the growth of IP televisions, eSports will increase its role as a major business area as well as cultural genre. With the growth of the number of online game players and fans, eSports will remain one of the most popular cultural activities among young people in Korea.

5

Professional Online Game Players as New Media Workers

Introduction

Over the last decade, "professional online game player" has become one of the most sought-after jobs for youth in Korea. With the rapid growth of knowledge-based information technologies, such as broadband, the Internet, and mobile phones, online gaming has become one of the most popular activities, and professional online game players—gamers who play each other for money rather than just on the computer for fun—have become an ever-increasing part of young people's day-to-day lives through televised online game competitions and game shows (Anderson, Funk, and Griffiths 2004; Whang 2003). The increasing popularity of online games and the emergence of professional online gamers in Korea is unique, because other countries do not have the same level of professional gaming and systematic professional online game competitions, although online games are becoming popular in many places. In Korea, where visual culture and new media are expanding rapidly, professional online game players (henceforth *pro gamers*) have quickly gained popularity among youth, and their cultural influence on young people cannot be disregarded.

As a reflection of the new pro-gamer phenomenon, pro gamers have been spotlighted as new celebrities, and pro gaming has become a new job category in Korea. A few pro gamers have been idolized as much as movie and music stars, making vast amounts of money and engaging in other activities deemed worthy of spectacle and intrigue by the general populace. Online gaming is no longer just trivial but has potential as a path for youth to become wealthy celebrities. The convergence of notions of culture with those of work heralds a new and important relation (McRobbie 2002, 97).

However, while online gaming has been a fantastic playground for a few skilled pro gamers, online gaming is not utopian for the majority of pro gamers and potential gamers. While a handful of pro gamers have fan clubs consisting of more than a half-million members and earn more than $200,000 per year, the majority of pro gamers and semipro gamers live a much less glamorous life, confronting hardships such as salaries lower than the national average and 14- to 16-hour days of training for two to three years (Canada Broadcasting Corporation 2007; Ku 2007). Many of these gamers have dropped out of high school to be pro gamers; what their futures hold is neither clear nor promising, even for top-level pro gamers.

Pro gamers are considered to be important components of Korea's digital economy and culture-driven Korean society. While several previous works analyzed general game players, including high school and college students, and there have been studies from a variety of perspectives and disciplines in terms of the health, behavior, and culture of general game players, there is a scarcity of systematic research on pro gamers. In fact, there are no academic papers analyzing pro gamers. This is a reflection of the occupation's comparatively recent entry into the cultural and media realms (Funk 2002; Kerr 2006a; Dyer-Witheford and de Peuter 2006). In fact, when Stephen Kline and others (2003, 198–199) published the first extensive analysis of the online game industry in 2003, the authors analyzed the labor issues of several kinds of game workers, including game testers, marketers, writers and editors of computer game magazines, box designers, and, most of all, workers in game development, all of whom had a wide variety of skills, security, and rewards. Aphra Kerr (2006a) discussed the demographics and characteristics of general game players by examining game preferences and the duration and frequency of play; however, neither work acknowledges the existence of pro gamers and their game world.

This chapter attempts to fill this research void. By employing a political economy approach, particularly a Marxian analysis on the issue of commodification (Marx 1867; Mosco 1996, 2009a; Grimes 2006), this chapter examines the working conditions of pro gamers as labor workers to determine their professional identities. This discussion includes several key issues: who these pro gamers are, how they became pro gamers, and what types of games they play. Exploring these characteristics provides a better understanding of pro gamers in Korea, particularly as a legitimate labor force in the realm of the new media. The chapter explores whether the pro gamers' world is full of existing labor issues, such as whether they experience exploitation as commodities or gendered environments. The chapter maps out the commodification process of pro gamers as part of professional game teams owned by media, telecommunications, and other big corporations. This investigation leads to a discussion of whether professional gaming—utilizing the combination of youth, talent, and culture in online gaming as in new media work—is a viable future for youth in the digital economy.

Professional Online Game Players as Knowledge-Based New Media Workers

It is challenging to determine pro gamers' characteristics as a labor force; new media and knowledge-based workers offer some similarities in their experience of work. Several scholars have analyzed the characteristics of online gamers—regular online game players, not pro gamers—as the labor force, and it is beneficial to start there (Yee 2006a, 2006b; Grimes 2006; Deuze, Martin, and Allen 2007).[1] Two previous works are especially useful in that they make clear connections between game play and work. Sara Grimes (2006, 983) first points out that "[unlike other sectors] online gaming has forced to blur the distinction between play and work by the digital game industry's own attempts, and the general game players have turned as workers whose major functions are subject to ferocious work conditions, such as arduous working hours and unhealthy working (playing) environments." Nick Yee (2006a, 69) also argues, "online games are inherently work platforms that train the general users to become better game workers because many players characterize their game play as a second job due to their addiction to the game." These works provide grounds to discuss online gaming as a workplace.

These contributions fall short of defining the real characteristics of professional gamers. What these debates lack is an analysis of the major trait of professional gaming: the money-making process. As Dallas Smythe (1981, 26) described, work should be defined as whatever one does for which one receives pay (e.g., wages, salaries). Therefore, it is arguable to posit general game players as the labor force, because their goal is not making money, while pro gamers are wage workers pursuing capital in the form of rewards and annual contracts. As Yeon Sung Choi, a former pro gamer who retired in 2007, states, "the happiest thing as a pro gamer is earning money through winnings" (Hua 2006). This assertion strongly claims that the most significant thing for pro gamers is to make money as businessmen and professional sports players, just as baseball and basketball players do. Their primary goal is to be better commodities, exchanged for capital based on privatized possession, as Karl Marx (1867) argued. Mia Consalvo (2007, 2) acknowledges that (general) game players have created different ways of playing and enjoying games, and such ways can give players a wider range of experiences and can reward superior players. However, she did not mean monetary reward as a form of wage or salary but rather as a form of recognition as a skilled player.

It is important to develop the discussion about whether pro gamers can be categorized in the realm of new media workers or knowledge-based information workers, or a combination of these two. With regard to the characteristics of new media workers, as Rosalind Gill (2002, 70) points out, in addition to generating capital through their labor, new media work is popularly regarded as exciting and cutting-edge, and its practitioners are seen as artistic, young, and cool—especially when compared to the previous generation of technologically literate IT workers, such as programmers and software designers. New media work, such as Web site design, digital animation, multimedia production, electronic artistry, Webcasting, and online game design, is a highly desired job for young people due to the creativity, flexibility in work hours, and high wages. Careers in postindustrial cultural fields such as gamework tend not to follow a neatly structured path; advancement tends to not be based on seniority, and career longevity is not guaranteed. Gamework is much more random, sporadic, and messy—a type of work and a kind of career that favors the young, single male (Deuze, Martin, and Allen 2007, 345; Dyer-Witheford and de Peuter 2006). As McRobbie (2002) argues, culture in this specific new media context refers to the creative, expressive, and symbolic activities in media, arts, and communicative practices, which demonstrate potential for gainful activity. Online gaming and online gamers are close to what McRobbie details because cultural and technical work are central to the Internet (Terranova 2000).

The definition of online gaming by the Korean government is not much different from this categorization. The government enacted the Advancement of Game Industry Act in 2006 to define the online game area and industry as part of its plan to support the games business legally and financially. According to the Act, the term *gamework* means visual content and apparatuses that have been manufactured in such a manner as to be played for amusement and additionally to help make good use of spare time and improve the effects of learning and physical exercise, using data-processing methods or devices, such as computer programs (Article 2). In this Act, the concept of visual content stems from a former Act that regulates music discs, films and video, and games, and it means literally and legally something recorded that can be replayed for audiences. Because the definition of *game* comes from the line of film, music disc, and animation, the Act considers online gamework as part of new media work.

Over the last two decades, the base of the global economy has changed from manual to knowledge work, and the center of gravity of a country's social expenditure has changed from goods to knowledge, as in several technology-driven countries, such as the United States and Japan. A knowledge-based workforce was seen as a major factor in the transition to a postindustrial economy and the ability for organizations to adjust to diversity, flexibility, and competition within the new knowledge economy (Drucker 1967, 364). As Drucker (1967, 264-65) argues, "the main investment, and the main product of the advanced economy should be in facilities which help develop a new class of workers who are able to deal with the ever changing diversity of knowledge-based computer applications."

Knowledge workers, in a narrow sense, are a group whose major function is the direct manipulation of symbols to create an original knowledge product, or to add obvious value to an existing one, as Richard Florida (2002) argues. According to this view, knowledge work would cover the labor of writers, artists, Web page designers, and software creators, which duplicates media workers. In fact, when Korea hosted the first WCG in 2001, President Kim Dae-Jung stated that online gaming and youth culture are a major part of the knowledge industry (Gamma 2001):

Cyber games are a business with high added value, based on knowledge and cultural creativity. It also serves as a link that interconnects young people of the world. I hope that the first WCG will help our nation to become recognized as one of the leaders in game, knowledge industry and information technology infrastructure, as well as help the world's game-loving young people exchange information and build friendships.

As Vincent Mosco (2009b) points out, the line between what is and is not creative labor in the knowledge field is fuzzy. Likewise, it is not clear whether pro gamers should be considered media workers and/or knowledge workers.

New media workers and knowledge-based workers have much in common, because their occupations involve making use of new technology and its convergence with new media, including the Internet and cable television. More importantly, pro gamers can be categorized as part of the media workers' industry, because the convergence of entertainment, new media, and technology is the major characteristic of pro gamers. The fact that some pro gamers eventually turn into professional game coaches, managers, television anchors, or commentators in the eSports area, and because pro gamers can become famous through new media such as cable television and the Internet, legitimates the categorization of pro gamers as new media workers. In addition, these jobs create and/or reflect contemporary youth culture, which has been one of the major values of media and/or knowledge workers. Therefore, it is reasonable to position pro gamers as a labor force comparable to media workers and/or knowledge workers who hold independent, creative, techno-savvy, and media-related jobs.

Social and Cultural Identities: The Lives of Online Pro-Gamers

"Online pro-gamer" has appeared as a job category for the first time in Korea in recent years. As a reflection of the short history of the pro-gamer phenomenon, there has been little to no study of pro gamers in terms of players' demographics, their playing patterns, and their identity and motivation for playing games. Because pro gamers did not exist until the mid-1990s, media or game scholars have not given specific attention to pro gamers as workers, let alone their cultural and economic characteristics, although they have studied amateur online game players as general youth who enjoy online games or video games. By nature, previous literature did not consider pro gamers as bona fide labor workers, because pro gamers were not a tangible body to analyze at that time. Determining pro gamers' major socioeconomic features, therefore, requires asking who they are, where they come from, how they are trained, how they organize their work across time and space, and how they get paid.

Online and professional gaming have been considered a great mix of culture and work for youth seeking knowledge work in Korea. Online gaming has increased in popularity, and this further entices players to choose gaming as a profession. Professional gaming has been recognized as an official job category in Korea (Macintyre 2000). The job opportunities that opened up with the expansion of the cultural sector resonate with the Korean government as it looks to achieve nearly full employment. Culture and work are critical to policy and thus to change. Since the late 1990s, work has been a site of endless government activity, including in Korea because many Korean youths want to get jobs in creative cultural industries (McRobbie 2002).

Pro gamers as the new media workforce are those who compete in online games and create income both directly and indirectly. Their demographics and characteristics are unique. Pro gamers are young, as they are 20.4 years old on average as of December 2006, and they work as pro gamers for only a couple of years (Korea Game Industry Agency 2007a). In 2005, about 39% of pro gamers were younger than 20 years old, and only 5% of pro gamers were over 25 years old (Samsung Economic Research Institute 2005b). In comparison, in the United States, the average (general) game player is 35 years old and has been playing for 13 years; about 40% of U.S. adults are regular game players (Entertainment Software Association 2007). In Korea, some of the (mostly male) pro gamers are starting their careers in their mid-teens and continue until their late twenties. However, they must stop their careers as pro gamers during their three years of compulsory military service. Although the Korean Air Force created its own professional game team in 2006, only a handful of gamers continue their work as part of this military team (Korea Game Industry Agency 2008b). After their military service, few players are able to return to the professional game world, because they cannot compete with younger players who have more agile and flexible fingers.

The number of pro gamers has rapidly increased over the last several years. Pro gamers are categorized as either regular pro gamers or semipro gamers. In 2001, when eSports began,[2] 131 regular pro gamers had registered after winning at least two official competitions as a member of an online game team, and there were 49 semipro gamers (figure 5.1). The total number of pro gamers soared to 950, including 450 pro gamers and 500 semipro gamers for 23 official games, as of December 2008 (*Electronic Daily 2009*). This number of online game players has surpassed that of professional baseball players in Korea. In 2007, there were 480 baseball players on eight professional teams (264 players) and eight semi-professional teams (216 players). Because there are hundreds of thousands of amateur online game players whose major goals are to become pro gamers, the overall number of pro gamers is expected to increase in the near future. For instance, when Samsung Electronics' KHAN, a professional game team, selected three intern gamers in 2005, more than 1,700 amateur players competed for the positions (Samsung Economic Research Institute 2005b). One survey reveals that pro gamer has become one of the most wanted jobs, along with firefighter, among elementary school students. The sociocultural influences of online pro-gamers, particularly on youth, are far beyond what the statistics explain.

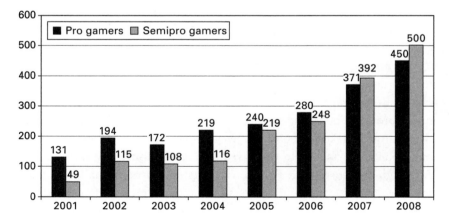

Figure 5.1
Change in the number of professional online gamers. *Source*: Data from Korea e-Sports Association 2009; *Electronic Daily* 2009.

Unlike other sports that have both male and female professional teams, such as basketball and volleyball, the professional gaming world includes both men and women, although it is full of young male players and female players are largely absent in the pro gamers world. This trend runs against the overall trend of the online game world, whose demographics are broadening. For example, the core gaming audience for television and live game shows, as well as game players in general, is made up, increasingly, of young women. According to Nexon, one of the leading online game publishers in Korea, three out of ten users of its *KartRider* game are women. In the case of NCsoft's *Lineage II* online game, women accounted for 18% of all players in 2003; this figure rose to 23.4% in 2004, 27.5% in 2005, and 27.6% in 2006 (Hwang 2007). In addition, dancing-themed and casual games, specifically designed and targeted at the female market, are gaining popularity. However, although women have crucial roles as viewers and as regular gamers, professional gaming is still a male-dominated category in Korea. Of 763 registered pro gamers as of June 2007, there were only 3 female pro gamers— Choi An-na, Lee Jong-mi, and Yeom Sun-hee (Ju 2007). In April 2009, when the Korea e-Sports Association started a new game league called Special Force Pro League,[3] Ongamenet SPARKYZ, a professional gaming team, organized a female-player-only team with five women players as part of its team for a FPS game (*Digital Times* 2009). Although a handful of these female gamers are challenging the stereotype of online pro gamers, it is still traditionally regarded as a domain for teenage boys (Hwang 2007), and it is not likely that there will be a large increase in the number of female pro gamers in the near future. In the early years of eSports (2001), there were more than 40 female players competing in the leagues; however, most of them disappeared because their skills were not competitive (*Yonhap News* 2002). As will be discussed, most male pro gamers work more than 13 hours per day in their dorms; however, female pro gamers do not undergo the rigors of team training, so several teams stopped hiring or supporting female players.

Two other major factors can be discussed as the major causes for the absence of female pro gamers. One factor is the value of male players as commodities. From the beginning, eSports has been dominated by male players, because corporations and media need them to appeal to young, female audiences who they are targeting as potential customers of their products. Online game teams emphasize sexy images of male players to attract mainly female fans. The other factor is the nature of the online games themselves, which tend to appeal more to men than to women. In fact, one of the major issues in eSports and for online game players is the lack of games that appeal to a wide audience; for example, *StarCraft* is based on a war scenario that male players prefer (Ju 2007). In Korea, as of June 2007, there were 27 competitive online games, including real-time simulation (*StarCraft*, *WarCraft 3*), FPS, sports, and racing games. There are no role-playing games, because players cannot finish them within the limited time needed for television shows (Korea Game Industry Agency 2007a). Because about 70% of pro gamers play *StarCraft* (because it is the most competitive and visual), which is primarily a game preferred by men, players who compete in other games have less opportunities to be star players, which has put female players at a disadvantage. As female pro gamer Lee Jong-mi (who has become a television master of ceremonies (MC) at OnMedia for online game shows since January 2009) claims, "online games need to be diversified in order to attract female players." While the numbers of female semipro gamers and/or intern players are gradually on the rise, the gender imbalance is still substantial (Ju 2007).

To identify their demographics and motivations for play, it is important to understand the ways in which amateur players turn into pro gamers. To graduate from an amateur player to a pro gamer in Korea, young players have to pass three rigorous and stressful stages. They must win at least two official competitions, and they must receive a general education organized by the Korea e-Sports Association. After the general education, they have to register as a pro gamer at the Association (Ha 2007a). Once this is done, they are a regular pro gamer. Semipro gamers have won at least one official game but are not registered yet. The final step to being a pro gamer is similar to that in other professional sports. There are twelve professional game teams in Korea, including the Korean Air Force team, and they select new pro gamers in several ways, including a draft system. There are two drafts every year, and the professional game teams can bid on the best amateur gamers who have passed the process above. As in many professional sports, professional game teams also scout some players from other professional teams in the middle of the season. Because many big corporations and media firms are interested in and invested in the game market these days, scouting has become a popular means of recruiting top players.

Another major sociocultural aspect of pro gamers is their daily activities. Almost all professional game teams have similar structures in terms of the number of players and training schedules and systems. Each team has, on average, 20 players, excluding semipro gamers and intern gamers. Most teams have their own dormitories and practice rooms in Seoul, where most professional games take place, and pro gamers live in their team's dormitory. For example, the team KTF MagicNs, which has the largest facilities, has two apartments as dormitories and one practice room in Seoul. Inside the camp, they sleep two or three players to a room. This means that about 10 players live in a 1,067-square-foot apartment. Professional teams support players by providing dormitories and practice rooms because some players come from areas with no money, and the boarding house system makes it easy for team managers and companies to manage team training and scheduling. However, the aims of corporations are obvious in that they need to create new commodities from the players as a medium to be used for sales of their services and goods.

It is also important to understand how pro gamers make money, because their earnings vary depending on their skills and popularity. Their earnings consist of annual salaries paid by professional game teams through contract (60%), awards from competition (27%), events (8%), and other sources (including advertising and book publication: 5%) (Samsung Economic Research Institute 2005b). The largest income opportunity for pro gamers is an annual salary from the professional team. The salary is determined when they secure a contract with a team. While a handful of famous pro gamers make more than $200,000 per year, based on their performance over time, the majority of pro gamers receive an annual salary of less than $10,000 per year (Ha 2007a). The second major source of earnings is winning a financial award during a competition. As of August 2005, pro gamers from 12 professional teams compete with each other in 21 games, including *StarCraft*, *WarCraft 3*, and *KartRider*, for $5 million in prize money annually (Korea e-Sports Association 2008b). Pro gamers also make some extra money through participating in events and advertising.

Pro gamers are cultural icons in the digital society, because pro gamers, particularly star players, are celebrities in Korea. They publish auto-biographies in their early and mid-twenties, they have fan autograph-signing events, and they have game shows in several corporations, as though they were movie and/or sports stars. In fact, famous pro gamers are besieged by fans seeking autographs. These young, boyish-looking pro gamers have achieved a level of fame bestowed elsewhere on movie idols, soccer stars, and Olympic champions. Each one of these star players has between 600,000 and 900,000 members in his fan club, and a celebrity pro gamer can make around $200,000 a year in salary and winnings combined, in a country where the average annual income is $16,291 (Hua 2006). In Korea, pro gamers are stars comparable to television talents, movie actors, and professional sports players. Thus, Korean youth are crazy about being new celebrities in the online gaming field. There are many amateur players and many youth who want to work in this new area. The future of the professional gaming field is bright in terms of attracting youth.

Socioeconomic Challenges of Pro Gamers as New Labor Workers

Achieving pro-gamer status does not, of course, guarantee financial success or celebrity-level fame. While several top players have made a fortune, most of the pro gamers have no substantial earnings or fame. Pro gamers face other challenges as well, such as low job security, the risk of changes in their employment status when team ownership shifts, and commodification and/or exploitation.

Of these, the most significant issue is job security, because the majority of the pro gamers do not make the average national income and leave the game world shortly after their appearance. When eSports began in the late 1990s, as one pro gamer stated, only about 20 to 30 professional gamers made more money than ordinary salaried people in Korea. At that time, the average income of pro gamers was estimated at about $2,000 to $3,000 a month (Chang 1999). As Yo Hwan Lim, known as the Emperor of Online Games confessed in his biography, there was no contract money, no annual salary, and no coach when he became a pro gamer in 1999; what they earned was only through winning a monetary award (Lim, Y. 2007). With the increase in the number of game teams and professional game competitions, the average income of a few star pro gamers soared when the contract system was introduced. For example, when Lim contracted with SKT T1 in 2005, his contract was worth as much as $200,000, which was the highest thus far (Kim, M. K. 2005).

However, for the majority of pro gamers, the situation has not improved. Although they have become professional game team members, as of March 2005, about 72.4% of pro gamers earned less than $10,000 annually, 15% earned $10,000 to $30,000, and 5.5% earned $30,000 to $50,000. Only 3.1% of pro gamers earned more than $100,000 per year during 2005. In addition, several hundred players do not have teams, and they make money through 100 individual games annually (Jang 2007). With the involvement of large telecommunications and media corporations who want to utilize online gaming as their corporate business and marketing medium, the situation of pro gamers in terms of their annual income is getting better; however, pro gamers in game teams owned by small corporations experience a similar environment as they did several years ago. The career length of the majority of pro gamers is short; most pass into oblivion only two or three years after their appearance as pro gamers. Job security is a big issue for most pro gamers, because, after their careers as pro gamers are over in their mid- to late twenties, only a few become coaches or television broadcasters on game shows.

Pro gamers have less job security due to the frequent shift in the game teams' ownership structure. The professional game teams were owned by nonprofit or small corporations managed by coaches until the first several years of the twenty-first century; pro gamers originally pursued fun and skills, and winning competitions was more to prove a player's superiority in skills than to secure a monetary award.[4] However, due to the popularity of eSports and the rapid growth of online gamers and viewers, pro gamers have become lucrative commodities for many corporations; thus, several large corporations, including those based in electronics, telecommunications, new media, and online publishing have increasingly become major players in eSports. Because online gaming is considered cutting-edge new media that is central to youth culture, several big corporations have begun to join the league. For pro gamers, the change of team ownership from nonprofit to commercial corporations can be lucrative; however, frequent changes in team ownership have brought about another form of job insecurity for many pro gamers. Because commercial corporations are primarily interested in a few star players, the remaining team members experience greater job insecurity when team ownership shifts; this has resulted in further self-commodification, which means they have to work hard to survive as team members.

To illustrate the frequent changes in team ownership, consider that, in 2006, HwaSeung, one of the largest shoemakers in Korea, bought PLUS and changed its name to Lecaf OZ. The two online game cable television channels have also become major players by taking over previous noncorporate teams. MBC Game bought and turned POS into MBC Game Hero, and Ongamenet bought KOR and changed its name to Ongamenet SPARKYZ. Another media giant, CJ, took over G.O. and turned it into CJ ENTUS. Several major electronics and telecommunications corporations, such as Samsung Electronics (Samsung KHAN), SK Telecom (SK Telecom T1), Pantech (Pantech EX), and KTF (KTF MagicNs), own or financially support several professional games teams. Meanwhile, HanbitSoft, one of the leading online game producers and publishers, also established its own team, Hanbit STARS. Other teams include STX Soul and eNature TOP. Because new corporations used to select only top professional players from the previous team, many of professional players could not continue their work in new teams.

eSports' consulting company IEG took over eNature and changed it into eStro in 2006 (Jung, D. 2006). Wemade, an online game publisher whose online games include *Legend of Mir* and *Chungin*, took over Pantech EX to make Wemade Fox (Wemade 2007). The Korean Air Force formed its own electronic gaming team and has played in the league since 2006. Although the Air Force has recruited talented, progamers as support personnel for the development of war simulation programs, this decision to form an Air Force team meets the demand of online gamers who have asked for an alternate form of military service so that they could resume their jobs following military service without having lost their gaming skills (Jung, S. 2006). The Air Force team has benefited several players and expedited some new teams; whereas, in the past, many capable gamers gave up playing to fulfill Korea's military service requirement, which requires all able-bodied men over 20 to serve for 24 to 28 months. Many of the pro gamers are enrolled in a cyberuniversity where they major in game planning and other high-tech subjects. This option enables some pro gamers to postpone their mandatory military service (Hua 2006) and stay longer on their current team. Pro gamers are limited-term commodities, with little or no job security behind the spotlights and celebrity fame. While pro gamers are drawn to the autonomy, creativity, and excitement that jobs in these new media industries can provide, they should be aware of the high risks associated with this work (Neff, Wissinger, and Zukin 2005, 308).

The Commodification Process of Pro Gamers

Pro gamers are not exceptional in the commodification process. Due to the significant role of pro gamers as new cultural icons whose sociocultural influences on the younger generation are enormous, as well as the unique commercial effects of online games, several key corporate sectors, including telecommunications, online game publishers, media firms, and large conglomerates have rapidly invested and expanded their involvement in eSports. They have created their own online game teams or purchased existing teams in order to boost their corporate images and improve their marketing efforts by identifying themselves as supporters of youth culture and digital media.

These corporations' commercial gains through their online game teams are enormous. KTF, for example, the largest telecommunications firm in Korea, invested $4.5 million in its own online game team between 1999 and May 2005, and it is estimated that the company earned $46.8 million worth of marketing effects—the advertising effect based on the team's exposure to the press and its participation in marketing events (Ku 2007). Driven by KTF's huge success, its rival SK Telecom, the country's top wireless carrier, launched the T1 team in April 2004, which includes Yo-Hwan Lim, one of the most popular *StarCraft* players. SK Telecom invested only $2 million and it was estimated to have earned $15 million worth of market effects through May 2005 (Kim, J. H. 2005). In addition, the CJ group announced that it earned more than 500% public relations effects through its online game team (CJ ENTUS). Between April 2006 and January 2007, the CJ group invested less than $2 million into CJ ENTUS, and the group earned $13.2 million worth of public relations effects (Lee, T. 2007).

Stimulated by these successes, several corporations, particularly tele-communications and media firms, have jumped into the online game business, because the young game fan demographic attracts handset makers and wireless operators because they are also the mobile phone companies' main customers (Kim, T. 2005). With the boom of eSports, star players have accumulated hundreds of thousands of fans, and the increase in the number of fans directly influences companies who own online game teams. For example, as of May 2005, Yo-Hwan Lim had 650,000 fan club members, exceeding Boa (460,000) and Hyo-ri Lee (370,000), two of the most famous female Korean singers (Kim, J. I. 2005). Corporations increase their brand names among fan club members and general audiences watching game shows on television. For these corporations, pro gamers are lucrative new commodities representing their corporate brands and goods, and the corporations have rapidly utilized these new commodities.

More specifically, the commodification of pro gamers begins with the capitalist's purchase of the commodified labor power and the means of production for exchanges for profit on the basis of privatized possessions (Coleman and Dyer-Witheford 2007). In this regard, Vincent Mosco (2009a, 132) claims, "commodification refers to the process of turning use values into exchange values, of transforming products whose value is determined by their ability to meet individual and social needs into products whose value is set by what they can bring in the marketplace." As such, pro gamers as workers are "made to exchange their labor power for a wage that does not compensate fully for the labor sold. The commodity labor is reproduced through processes of absolute (extending the working day) and relative (intensification of labor process) exploitation that intensify the extraction of surplus value" as Marxian theory states (Mosco 1996, 142).

Pro gamers' participation in online game competitions is commodified and marketed as both a paid-for leisure experience (through competition) and as a key selling point of corporations having game teams (Grimes 2006). The pro gamer's world shows the process of commodification of Karl Marx (1867). Pro gamers enjoy their use value for fun with high-level game skills, which means pro gaming remained simple because it was tied to its use-value pursuing trivial fun; however, they immediately turned into exchange value backed by corporations whose major goal is to make surplus through the commodification process of pro gamers.

Because pro gamers have value to their organizations, corporations owning the professional game teams have developed sophisticated commodification strategies by adopting a star-making process, as some film producers create superstars. Because the images of the pro gamers affects the images of companies and the sales of the goods of those companies, corporations train pro gamers not only as players but also as good people to be respected. The star-making process is rigorous, because these corporations strictly control pro gamers' daily lives through their team managers and coaches. Pro gamers have a tight and hard schedule to prepare for competitions. Ongamenet team players, owned by a cable broadcasting firm, have only one day off per week, for example, and they stay at the dormitory for practice. Unpleasantly, in order to avoid getting muscle cramps due to long practice, the pro gamers' practice room in their dormitory is always hot and without air conditioning. The hard regimen can take its toll, even on young players in their early twenties. While enjoying celebrity acclaim, some star players avoid going out, and, when they do go out, they put their heads down—to dodge the whispers, the stares, and the pleas for autographs from adoring fans. Such are the hardships of celebrity pro gamers in Korea, where cultural industries are now so central to local and national economics and culture (Hua 2006).

In reference to the star-making process of commodification, Hun-Ho Je, director of the Korea e-Sports Association, states, "players must maintain old-fashioned decorum. They cannot sweat and get angry, or get drunk, whether they are competing or not. We make them into gentlemen. Now they train [to be] happy when they win a game" (Hua 2006). Oh Sun, manager of the CJ professional game team also points out, "we spend about $200,000 to operate the team per month, so players must practice for 13-14 hours on average. Since dating with girl friends also bothers practice, we prohibit players from dating" (Ku 2007).

When the professional league started, Samsung—the largest conglomerate in Korea—also participated in eSports, putting its team members into an apartment in downtown Seoul where they were trained, ate, and slept together five days a week, much as Korean Olympic athletes practice together before the Olympic Games. Drinking and smoking were strictly forbidden. Pro gamers rose at 6 a.m. and headed to the gym for an hour-long workout. After some cornflakes and fried eggs back at the apartment, they watched playbacks of games to study moves, and performed finger exercises to improve their agility. Pro gamers practiced all day, spending up to 13 hours a day learning the intricate features of *StarCraft*, their specialty and a hugely popular game in Korea (Macintyre 2000). Unlike other professional team owners, Samsung uses their players to test products under development, including both games and hardware (Macintyre 2000), which is another example of the commodification of pro gamers; that is, through the extra work they must do. Because these corporations support only a handful of star players, their investment in the welfare of the other team members is paltry. As one online game designer (Cho, S. 2005) stated, "large corporations consider eSports as part of their marketing strategies depending on a few star players. They are reluctant to invest in the teams for the long run; instead of supporting new players, they want to have one or two existing pro gamers as a public relation strategy." The star-making process is no more than the commodification of pro gamers. Excessive practicing hours are enforced for a variety of reasons. While several teams force pro gamers to work hard to compete with other teams' players, pro gamers are afraid of being left behind. Their competitors are not only other teams' players, but also new pro gamers moving up from the amateurs, intern players, and semipro gamers. They are all potential competitors, and the players acknowledge that being a pro gamer is more difficult than winning official competitions.

An additional factor is the volatility of the industry (Dyer-Witheford and de Peuter 2006, 611). Because online game teams change hands rapidly, pro gamers have to be prepared for this swift change in ownership structure. Pro gamers are usually only in their late teens or early twenties. They feel that being a good commodity through winning competitions is the one way to secure their job in the midst of the change of the owners of their teams; therefore, they have to work hard. For these reasons, pro gamers accept their commodification with no resistance. As Nick Dyer-Witheford and Greig de Peuter (2006) argue, general game workers (other than pro gamers), such as game designers and producers, sometimes try to resist the hard regimen of the industry and the commodification of their labor force, for example, through the unionization of workers; however, the young pro gamers never look back, and in some senses, they are training themselves to be more valuable commodities. One semipro gamer states, "I have dreamed of being a pro gamer since my 5th grade. Although the all day practice is sick and tired, there is nothing to go, and nothing to do else" (Ha 2007b).

These days, many companies have benefited from the convergence of technology, culture, and youth, not only in production, but also in consumption. Corporations in telecommunications, media, and online publishing have deliberately organized this convergence as part of their marketing strategies. As many scholars claim, a crucial aspect of the transition from Fordism (which emphasized mass production, and mass production through standardization) to post-Fordism (which relied on information technologies and flexible labor markets) has been the capitalist shift in emphasis from material to experiential goods, expanding markets for incessantly exhausted and renewed entertainment commodities that penetrate into every available space and moment of everyday life (cited by Kline (2003)). In this regard, Dan Schiller (2007) analyzes pro gamers as paid workers and audiences as unpaid labor, together having been commodified by corporations who own eSports teams, which has resulted in the integration of production and consumption in a new digital economy. On the one hand, youthful enthusiasm, cool and creative culture, high skills, and the new media environment represent the professional gaming world, while, on the other hand, high stress levels, job insecurity, and commodification are part of pro gamers' socioeconomic lives.

Summary

This chapter investigates the characteristics of pro gamers as new media workers to explore pro gamers as a legitimate labor force. The growth of eSports allowed pro gamers to get established. As a reflection of eSports' popularity, those who excel in digital play are highly regarded. Players involved in professional gaming are often celebrities supported by major corporate sponsorship and enthusiastic and loyal fans. Many young Koreans aspire to be pro gamers, and this admiration contributes to the existing national passion for games.

The recent developments investigated herein are evidence of professional gaming's significance as a new job category in the digital society. The pro gamers share much with new media workers—informal and creative work full of young, diverse types who are the epitome of cool

(Gill 2002). The demand for cultural goods on an ever-increasing scale brings into being new kinds of labor markets and new kinds of work (McRobbie 2002). In Korea, where cultural forces, such as film, television programming, and game software are now so central to local and national economies, the convergence of youth, talent, culture, and technology is an excellent opportunity for digital Korea, not only through job opportunities but also as image-makers for society (McRobbie 2002). Success, wealth, and even fame and celebrity are now routinely offered to those prepared to take the risks and put in the long hours that professional gaming demands.

However, there are downsides to professional gaming. This chapter addresses the lack of job security, low pay, long hours of practice, gender issues, and the commodification of players. What one must understand is that pro gamers as new media workers are permanently transitional workers, requiring risk-taking activity and high degrees of mobility from the workforce (McRobbie 2002). After only a couple of years, pro gamers have to leave the professional online game world because newer, younger players with higher skills emerge. As a result, pro gamers experience the shortest job career period among professionals (e.g., sports, dance, singing, and filming). Where the speed of keyboarding is a key component, late twenties are retirement ages for most pro gamers; their skills lag far behind youth in their late teens and early twenties, so they cannot win the competitions. Although some pro gamers are making a fortune and gaining national fame, their labor power has been one of the most significant commodities in the digital economy.

In sum, as Bernard Miege (1989) argues, social and cultural capital is being created, commodified, and consumed in these new media workers. Culture as a way of life was deeply embedded in social institutions and practices; now, as a way of earning a living, it is increasingly disembedded, rapidly disconnected from any notion of vernacular as soon as its potential for commodification is spotted (McRobbie 2002). Pro gamers will continue to participate in their own commodification in the midst of the growth of youth culture, because both pro gamers and online teams whose mother companies are megatelecommunications and media corporations promote the commodification process, and audiences consume brand images of professional game teams and the corporations that own and finance them.

6

Online Game Fans: New Audience Commodities in the New Media Era?

Introduction

Yeon Sung Choi, one of the most famous pros, wearing a NASCAR-style costume, sits at a computer station on a stage for a live television game competition in the Ongamenet Studio in Seoul, Korea, on June 7, 2007. Choi is a pro-gamer on an SKT T1 team, and he nervously but strongly hits the keyboard. The contest begins with his opponent, Chae Ho Lee, of MBC Game Hero, in a *Star-Craft* game at another computer station on the same stage. … It is a computerized online battle, projected onto a screen for some 500 spectators who are physically present, and broadcast over cable television for millions of fans. Whenever his fingers move to defeat his opponent, the audience, primarily composed of fan club members, cheers loudly while enthusiastically waving their placards and a yellow ribbon symbolizing Choi. He has 900,000 members in his fan club. (Jin's observations at the studio in 2007)

The rapid growth of online gaming and the boom of eSports have relied heavily on the increasing number of online game users, and most importantly on the existence of game fans. Every day, hundreds of thousands of people, mainly teens and those in their early twenties, spend a lot of money and time on online gaming. Watching online game competitions between professional online game players on television has also become a major cultural and entertainment activity among Korean youth. With the rapid penetration of broadband services, more Internet users are enjoying online games, while many young online game fans enjoy watching online game competitions on cable television and Internet television. They also frequently visit several leagues in game studios to support their favorite professional game players. In Korea, a few pro gamers have fan clubs easily exceeding 500,000 fans. These fans have produced a new Internet culture, which is unique due to the increasing number of fan club members, comparable to fan clubs for television and movie stars.

Despite their economic and cultural significance, rapid growth, and widespread appeal in Korea, online game fan culture and fan economy, particularly from a critical perspective, has received scant attention from media researchers. While several previous articles have analyzed online gaming from a cultural studies perspective, the articles did not emphasize the fact that the fan culture in the online game sector is different from the fan culture in the movie and music industries, because the most popular online game teams and pro gamers are commercially owned by corporations, including telecommunications, media, and electronics companies, and they work for corporate interests.

In particular, it is rare to see an analysis of the relationship between online game fans, professional teams and pro gamers in the context of commodification, although the game fans' participation in online game shows and fan club meetings are commodified and marketed as both a paid-for leisure experience and as a key selling point of corporations that own game teams. More importantly, audiences buy goods and spend their income accordingly. Corporations owning online game teams clearly understand what they sell to ever-increasing audiences that represent all socioeconomic classes; they are selling not only goods and services but also their brands in the long run. The most important thing for those corporations is that audiences get used to their brand name.

This chapter analyzes the commodification process of online game fans and discusses the ways in which companies that own professional game teams have benefited from the convergence of technology, culture, and youth, not only in production but also in consumption. More specifically, it maps out how corporations (including telecoms, media, and online publishers) have deliberately organized this convergence as part of their marketing strategies, which has become a new audience commodity process. In addition to the political economy approach, the discussion in this chapter is partially based on interviews conducted with online game fans and game managers from both online game show networks and online game teams in Seoul, Korea, between summer 2007 and January 2009. In June 2007, interviews were conducted in Seoul at live online game competitions and live competition shows organized by Ongamenet.

Audience Commodity in Online Gaming

Pro gamers and online game fans are latecomers in the realm of the digital economy and digital culture. However, in Korean society, pro gamers are some of the most famous celebrities, as discussed in chapter 5, and young game fans have become an emerging target audience. In particular, online game fans are specific target customers for several major telecommunications and media corporations due to their purchasing power and their rapid acceptance of new media. Although the commodification process of movie and sports stars and their fans is not new, a growing interest in fan communities as new kinds of participatory cultures is evident through online gaming. Fan communities also constitute target audiences that big corporations would like to actively commodify.

As Vincent Mosco (1996, 2009a) claims, the process of commodification in general is as follows: use-value is determined by a product's ability to meet individual and social needs, whereas exchange-value is determined by what a product can bring to the marketplace. Commodification occurs when use-value is transformed into exchange-value. Taking this for granted, the commodification process of pro-gamers and online game fans is the embodiment of the audience commodity, as discussed by Dallas Smythe (1981). Smythe recognized the economic relationship between the advertiser and the corporate product sponsor—the commodity producers pay advertising agencies for the advertiser's product: for example, a broadcast commercial, a published ad, or a billboard. He also identified that the source of profit for the corporate product depends on whether "audience response results in the ringing of cash registers where the sponsor's product is sold to the ultimate producer" (Smythe 1951). Several theoreticians, including John Fiske (1989) and Henry Jenkins (1992) have celebrated fan practices as a kind of oppositional culture (Theberge 2005). For Fiske, popular culture is, by definition, of the people, and it works against commodification (Fiske 1989). Jenkins (1992) also presents a well-argued case that fans are active participants in a burgeoning underground of cultural consumerism as owners, which means the fan community sees itself in opposition to the capitalist control of culture, and they have begun to impact the original producers. He defines so-called participatory culture as one with relatively low barriers to artistic expression, with strong support for creating and sharing one's creations with others and where members feel some degree of social connection with one another, while the community itself provides strong incentives for creative expression and active participation (Jenkins 2006, 7). Participatory media technologies like the Internet and online game engines have permitted fans to broadcast their own unofficial and unlicensed additions, thus changing the political economy of media irrevocably and for the better (Jenkins (2006), cited by Nakamura (2009)).[1] In the contemporary context, however, the fan clubs appear to operate in a more complex modality, with fan interests and industry interests feeding off and reinforcing each other, rather than acting in opposition (Theberge 2005).

In 1977, Smythe more fully articulated his theory of audience-as-commodity, although still conceiving of audience time as commodity. Smythe (1977) wanted to understand what the commodity form of mass-produced, advertiser-supported communications under monopoly capitalism was. The materialist answer is audiences, including readerships (Artz 2008). Under contemporary capitalism, Smythe argues:

All non-sleeping time of most of the population is work time. This work time is devoted to the production of commodities in general (both where people get paid for their work and as members of audiences) and in the production and reproduction of labor power (the pay for which is subsumed in their income). Of the off-the-job work time, the largest single block is time of the audiences which is sold to advertisers. It is not sold by workers but by the mass media of communications. (Smythe and Guback 1994)

Smythe indeed observed that audiences were products that commercial networks sold to corporate advertisers. He recognized that audiences were subjected to programming that was produced, distributed, and promoted to meet the interests of advertisers who ultimately funded private television and developed media technology for profit. The audience's relationship and interaction with the media as a continuum, which departs from the audience's entertainment and eventually becomes an advertiser's commodity, is related to the media (Grimes 2006). In this regard, Smythe (1981, 222) claimed:

In economic terms, the audience commodity is a non-durable producers' good which is bought and used in the marketing of the advertiser's product. The work which audience members perform for the advertiser to whom they have been sold is learning to buy goods and to spend their income accordingly. ... In short, they work to create the demand for advertised goods which is the purpose of the monopoly-capitalist advertisers.

In other words, "the audience was not simply passing time; it was also spending time in fairly regimented ways with advertising-supported media as the focus of attention (attention to a program), or as the focus of socializing" (like going to a film together) (Meehan 1993, 382). As Lazzarato (1996) claims, leisure time and working time are increasingly fused, making life inseparable from work. However, audiences have more or less value depending on their demographics and the value of those demographics to particular product producers: denture manufacturers value viewers over 50, candy manufacturers prefer younger viewers, beer producers target males 21 to 34, and so on (Artz 2008). Corporations, such as telecommunications, media, and online publishers, have utilized the younger generation (the majority of pro-gamer fan club members) because they tend to accept new technology rapidly and are heavy users of new media.

Online Game Fandom

Online gaming has increased in popularity and has further enticed new players to choose gaming as a profession. This is a new burgeoning area, which has expanded rapidly in recent years—one that is also constantly renewing itself in response to changing technologies, including high-speed Internet. The developments of the Internet and broadband are crucial for online gaming because they have changed fan cultures and fan economy. Recent developments in media economy and media technology suggest a shift of growing interactivity in audience practices and growing interest in fan communities as new kinds of participatory cultures (Nikunen 2007, 111). Because online gaming is a major part of the Internet, and online game fans partially live in cyberspace, it is important to understand online game fandom to be able to better understand online gaming, fan culture, and the digital economy.[2]

The rise of fan culture is intimately bound up with the creation of the star-making system in popular culture. Indeed, they are inextricably linked; without the artificial buildup of star personae, there would be insufficient focus for the fan's desire. In media studies, the rise of the star system is usually associated with the development of the film industry during the early years of the twentieth century (Theberge 2005, 486). Because of their potential to affect the images of companies and the sale of the goods of those companies, producers and managers strictly controlled movie and television stars' daily lives. Online gaming is not much different, as discussed in chapter 5. During interviews conducted in Seoul, Korea, in June 2007, one college student succinctly explained the future of online gamers and eSports: "there are many amateurs and many youth who want to work in this new area. The future is bright in terms of attracting youth. They want to have their jobs while enjoying themselves. In this regard, pro gamers will be some of the most fascinating people for youth" (Jin 2007, interview subject 1). As such, people, particularly young people, are exceptionally ardent about games, not only enjoying online games but also wanting to become pro gamers.

Fan clubs have long been a feature of both the cinema and record industries, although neither industry has pursued them as a regular avenue of profits, preferring to leave their organization and activities in the hands of fans themselves. In the case of online gaming, with the rise of the Internet and eSports, fans have, from the outset, engaged in a variety of online discussions related to their interests. What is of interest in this context is the transformation, from fan club members to customers, of those other, more-or-less organized, official fan clubs, where the tensions between fandom and organized consumption are most evident (Theberge 2005, 486).

In Korea, fan culture in online gaming has developed primarily through fan clubs organized by members. In the broadcasting and movie sectors, fan club members organize meetings and rallies to support their favorite stars through the telephone and newspapers, and later through the Internet; from the outset, online game fan clubs utilized the Internet to organize. They have opened their online fan cafés in cyberspace, particularly at the largest Web portals, including Daum and Naver. These fan cafés are important to fan culture, because they are places where fans learn about fan meetings and pro gamers' game schedules. Fan club members have their own Web sites to connect with other members. With the rise of cross-platforming and convergent media through Web 2.0, the role of online communities has been critical (Hjorth and Chan 2009). As the Internet is rapidly transformed from the relatively disorganized activity of the early days to the browser-mediated Web boom of the

1990s (Theberge 2005), and further to its connection to social networking systems in the twenty-first century, the degree to which conventional fan club activity has shifted to Web 2.0 is remarkable. In Korea, the largest fan cafés are in Daum. Through their fan club sites, fans organize several significant events, including meetings at the game stadium to cheer for their favored pro-gamers. With the blooming of eSports, star players have hundreds of thousands of fans, and the increase in the number of fans and fan clubs directly influences companies who own online game teams.

For example, the fan Web site with the most members (more than 600,000) in Korea is not for a sex-symbol pop singer but for Yo-Hwan Lim, a pro-gamer. For comparative purposes, the number of pro-gamer fan clubs is far greater than those of movie, music, and sports stars in Korea. Yo-Hwan Lim has 650,000 fan club members, exceeding Boa (460,000) and Hyo-ri Lee (370,000), two famous Korean singers (Kim, J. I. 2005). Yo-Hwan Lim's fan club members numbered only 140,000 as of July 2002, and his fan club membership soared to as many as 900,000 for a while in 2005 and 2006. According to the Daum Café, which created fan cafés first, Yo-Hwan Lim had the largest number of fan club members at 500,692 as of January 23, 2009, compared to Boa (361,630), Big Bang (most popular music group in 2008: 359,676), and Ji-Sung Park (the most popular soccer player: 87,279) (table 6.1). Several top pro-gamers also have more than 200,000 fans; their popularity is much higher than that of other celebrities.[3] Corporations naturally plan to increase the visibility of their brand names among increasing fan club

Table 6.1
Number of Fan Club Members

Name	Area	Number
Lim Yo-Hwan	Pro gamer	500,692
Boa	Singer	361,630
Big Bang	Singer	359,676
Bae Yong Jun	Actor	202,411
Lee Yun Yul	Pro gamer	146,526
Park Ji Sung	Professional soccer player	87,279
Lee Yo Lee	Singer	43,932

Source: http://www.daum.net (January 23, 2009).

members and general audiences watching game shows on television by aligning their companies with pro gamers.

More specifically, Yo-Hwan Lim's fan café at Daum (http://cafe .daum.net/yohwanfan) includes several important features, including a current tally of fan club members. The fan café consists of three major areas, including the Member Room, Yo-Hwan Room, and Data Room. Each room is organized and managed by fan club members. The Member Room has several categories, such as free talk, member pictures, cheer board, and attendance check. The Yo-Hwan Room consists of Yo-Hwan's writings, schedule, post-game, and pictures. Under Data Room, there are several categories, including one with replays of Yo-Hwan's games, which enables fans to access his previous games. Fan cafés encourage online game fans to email their comments and pictures taken during online games in the game studio. Such developments deploy the umbrella promise of interactivity, which develops new forms of consumption (Sterling 2005). The Yo-Hwan Cheer Board is also critical to connect fans with the player. In this category, fans are able to create their own cheer boards. The café organizers select the best cheer board among those uploaded and put it next to the monitor in the game studio so that fans in the studio can see it.

Cable television's broadcast of a made-for-television eSports league seems to be as much a game show as an athletic event. Stagehands call for applause after commercial breaks, and more than 500 fans—most of them clutching thundersticks like those found at basketball games—sit in bleachers inside the game studio. The on-site fans loudly encourage their favorite team. Whenever there are games in game studios at either Ongamenet or MBC Game, hundreds of young people, mostly women and girls who are fan club members of professional players, wave signs and sing slogans as they swirl in the glare of klieg lights. It is the kind of fan frenzy that anywhere else would be reserved for rock stars or movie legends (Schiesel 2006).

Fan club culture, which relies on the Internet to unite far-flung viewers in ongoing events and to critique an increasing number of online games, provides both information and feedback on matches. For example, during the post-game period, fan members and players provide their own opinions on the game. Many of those who visit the café are convinced that their feedback has had some sort of impact on pro gamers for their next games (Sterling 2005).

Another famous pro gamer, Yon Yeol Lee, also has five fan cafés, including in Daum and Cyworld. One of the smallest fan cafés (http://www.leeyoonyeol.com/) has been popular, and as many as 1,200 members regularly update their cheer letter to Lee. These fan letters are widely read by other fan club members as well as players. Given that Korea's young generation is keen toward new media, particularly the Internet, fan club activities and/or participation are getting more popular in Korea. In 2005, when two telecommunications rival teams, SK Telecom and KTF MagicNs, met for the championship game, players on each team had about 1 million fan club members. As such, eSports had already become one of the most popular sports and entertainment forms for 15 million Korean people in the same year (Kim, D. 2005).

Fan clubs are important when fans visit game stadiums and cheer for their favorite players; they do these activities based on fan clubs. Through a fan club café, they announce players' schedules and ask the fans to visit on site, particularly for big games. Several fan club members meet before the games and prepare several placards as in many professional sports games. Because the studio is not that big, fan club members from different cafés sit together and wave their placards. One fan club member of Yeon Sung Choi, who was interviewed in summer 2007, explained that many fan club members are die-hard fans:

Through our visits, several fan club members have become friends. Although our ages are different, from high school students to late 20s, we share common interests, one being our favorite player. Before visiting the game studio, some of us meet to make placards and talk on the telephone to arrange our seats. There are about 500 audience members present for big games, and they cheer for their favorite players with other fan club members. There are more than 10 fan clubs for each famous player, and there are many subgroups. (Jin 2007, interview subject 2)

Another fan club member of Yeon Sung Choi, who is a college student, explains that most colleges, particularly in the Seoul metropolitan area, have many fan club members:

Several friends of mine are also fan club members at the same university. Sometimes, we play together for fun at PC cafés, and we visit the game studio once a month to watch and cheer Yeon Sung Choi. During our visits, we learn several strategies for *StarCraft* while enjoying games. Fan club activities are among the most important parts of our college life. (Jin 2007, interview subject 3)

In fact, online game fandom requires a serious investment of time. Many fan club members create their own cheer boards as well as a Web site as a symbolic gesture of their support to pro gamers. Even though this is a pleasant type of participation, this kind of voluntary involvement has turned into the commodification process, because corporations and advertising agencies utilize fans' efforts and time for profit. Fan club members collectively put a significant amount of time and energy into the creation of their fandom. Of course, many fan club members devote time not just to watching and visiting game competitions but also to gathering information about their favorite players to share. As Tiziana Terranova (2000) claims, it is a good example of the free labor characteristic, which means that online game fans provide their labor without an exchange of money or wage. In contrast to online fan members for television shows, including Television Without Pity, which provides instant feedback to television writers and scriptwriters for production (Andrejevic 2008), online game fan clubs do not provide any direct suggestions to improve the game competition due to the fact that pro gamers cannot read and think about what fans want in the midst of their games.

However, fans' activities, which are free labor, certainly provide some energies and strategies for future games. Online game fan club members provide some feedback to eSports by developing their own forums, sometimes organized by themselves or by other eSports-related agencies. Online game fans' leisure is being commodified by the game industry, because they exploit the modders. As Julian Kucklich (2005) states, the relationship between work and play is changing, leading, as it were, to a hybrid form of "playbour." Game fans and players, as modders who conduct computer game modification, are an important part of gaming culture as well as an increasingly important source of value for the game industry because they, as a form of unpaid labor, add a considerable amount of value to commercial games (Postigo 2003). Arguably, the precariousness of modders' playbour lies in the fact that it is simultaneously voluntarily given and unwaged, enjoyed, and exploited (Terranova 2000).[4]

In fact, in November 2005, the Korea e-Sports Association conducted a survey with 852 online game fan club members, which has resulted in the creation of a new team in the Air Force and the introduction of IP televisions as new channels for the growth of eSports (Yoon 2005). Several online game magazines and agencies also conduct surveys regularly to ask questions about fans' changing tastes for online gaming and eSports, including competition scheduling and methods; therefore, online game fan club members have influenced the change and continuity of online game culture. Online game fans' feedback proves that the games offer a glimpse of what might become a new breed of large-scale or massively social technologies (Fitzgerald 2005). The collective knowledge of large groups is often unrecognized and almost always undervalued by society. However, as James Surowiecki (2004) argues, many everyday activities, from voting in elections to the operation of the stock market, or even to the way Google locates Web pages, depend on the collective input and knowledge of large groups of people. Under the right conditions, crowds can act more wisely than an expert individual can. The ways technology might be used to support the development of smart crowds is a relatively unexplored area. Applications such as wikis and online games certainly show how large groups of people can interact online as well as offline (Fitzgerald 2005).

The rapid growth of game audiences and the associated cultural phenomena are unique to Korea. Game audiences are susceptible to adopting online gaming as the major part of their daily lives, formerly occupied by professional sports. As the World Cup soccer game held in Korea and Japan in 2002 proves, Korean youth like to watch the big events together to cheer national players. During the major games in 2002, more than 24 million people spontaneously participated in street rallies during the event in front of big television screens. Similarly, Korean youth want to express their support for their favorite pro-gamers both inside and out of the game studios. They have organized online fan clubs so they can connect with the online community, which has been turned into a commodity.

Online Gaming: Is This a New Area for the Commodified Audience?

Online game fans, particularly fan club members, have developed a new concept of fan culture. However, their unique fan culture has also been part of commodified culture due to the importance of online game fans for major telecommunications and media corporations. Online game fans are homogeneous in terms of their ages (teens and early twenties), gender (female), and education (high school or college students); therefore, for corporations, they are well-targeted customers that cannot be ignored. As one female game fan interviewed at Ongamenet Stadium in 2007 mentioned;

From the first instance, eSports has been dominated by male players because corporations and media need them to appeal to youth audiences. Online game teams emphasize sexy images of male players to attract mainly female fans. Although female players are gradually increasing, it does not change the map because male and female players have shown distinct skill gaps. So, their major target is male players, and the majority of fan club members are female, which is a great mix for corporations. (Jin 2007, interview subject 4)

The commodification process of pro-gamers and game fans, again, is the embodiment of the audience commodity discussed by Dallas Smythe (1981). In fact, online game competitions draw hundreds of thousands of avid fans (*active audience*, to use Smythe's term) who watch on massive indoor screens, or on one of two game-only cable channels broadcasting 24 hours a day. Again, the audience's relationship and interaction with the media as a continuum, which departs from the audience's entertainment and eventually becomes an advertiser's commodity, is related to the media (Grimes 2006).

Commodification of the pro-gamers is indeed evident. Several large conglomerates, including telecommunications, online publishing, and media firms, have invested in eSports due to online gaming's enormous commercial effects. Again, there are twelve professional online game teams primarily owned by big corporations (Samsung Electronics), telecommunications (KTF, SKT), and media (MBC, CJ). These major corporations have invested and/or expanded their investments in eSports because of the potential benefits from the digital culture and economy. Their investments have been successful in terms of raising corporate images and revenues.

As noted in the previous chapter, KTF, one of the largest telecom firms, which merged with KT in 2009, invested $4.5 million in its own online game team, MagicN's, between 1999 and May 2005, and it is estimated that the company earned $46.8 million worth of marketing effects—the advertising effect based on the team's exposure to the press and its participation in marketing events. Driven by KTF's huge success, its rival SK Telecom, the country's top wireless carrier, launched the T1 team in April 2004, which includes Yo-Hwan Lim, one of the most popular *StarCraft* players. SK Telecom invested $2 million and was estimated to have earned $15 million worth of market effects through May 2005 (Kim, J. H. 2005). Although they sold their own online game team (Pantech EX) to Wemade in 2007, Pantech, Korea's third-largest cell phone maker, enjoyed an increase in the sales of its new handset when it owned Pantech EX. As the company claims, consumers and online fan clubs themselves are their publicity agents, because tech-savvy fans spread the word of new mobile phones (Kim, S. 2004). Samsung Electronics, the world's third-largest handset manufacturer, established its gaming team, KAHN, in 2000. The eSports blitz is becoming much more serious between mobile carriers.

As these examples prove, several corporations, particularly in telecommunications, have jumped into the online game business because the game fan demographic attracts the products of handset makers and wireless operators, because young fans are also the mobile phone company's main customers (Kim, T. 2005). Cell phone makers and mobile operators have gone all-out to win the support of online game fans in their late teens or early twenties. In Korea, mobile phone products are primarily targeted at teenagers (Yoon 2006). Because they will also be major consumer group members in the near future, it is critical to attract them with corporate marketing strategies. In fact, 41.7% of teens and people in their twenties bought or received their first mobile phone during their elementary years, and another 41.7% of them bought them during their middle school years, particularly between sixth and seventh grades in Korea (*Game Chosun* 2008). Because they also started to enjoy online gaming in their early years, they are naturally becoming online game fans and are major target customers for mobile phone makers and telecommunications companies.

In the case of the broadcasting and film industries, fans of stars are diverse in terms of gender, age, and education, and their favorite stars do not belong to any corporate-owned teams. In contrast, in eSports, pro gamers are part of online game teams that major telecommunications and media corporations own. These corporations naturally benefit from pro-gamers and online gaming and consequently commodify the customers, game fans, and, most of all, fan club members, who are the major target customers. For these corporations, fans are the new economy, because fans do not just buy their products, they convince their friends to give them a try. General customers come and go easily. However, fans fight for the survival of the online game teams; therefore, they also fight for the survival of the corporations (Caddell 2008).

As such, the corporations' aims are obvious in the sense that they have created new commodities, not as goods to be directly sold but as a medium to be used for the sales of their services and goods.[5] More specifically, again, corporations such as telecommunications, media, and online publishers have deliberately organized this convergence as part of their marketing strategies, which is a new audience commodity process developed from a television audience commodity concept. The mobile-phone-related companies have particularly jumped onto the gaming bandwagon to jazz up their images by exerting a strong pull on online game fans. As one stock analyst explains, "the game fan demographic attracts handset makers and wireless operators because the young fans are also the mobile phone outfits' main customers" (Kim, T. 2005). Mobile phone operators also develop new strategies to utilize online game fans. They acknowledge that most young Koreans have handsets, so they deliver video games to handsets, allowing users to play games. SK Telecom and KTF launched phone-based game services in April 2005. KTF made a deal with online game developer CJ Internet Corporation to purchase game content for their handsets in 2004 (Kim, T. 2005).

Advertising and Audience Commodity

Advertising agencies and large corporations have rapidly utilized online fan clubs, which are valuable commodities as major Internet advertising resources. Pro gamers are effective in terms of their exposure to fans and general audiences, and, because they are able to wear sponsors' hats, clothes, and shoes, they are significant commodities for advertising agencies. Due to increasing demands, several online game developers use specific brands, including clothes, cars, and handsets for the games and players to attract online game viewers and fans. As many movies and television programs utilize product placement to search for additional sources of revenue (Wasko 1994), online gaming has been a new source of advertising, which has resulted in the commodification of audiences.

In the realm of online gaming, there are several types of game advertising, including static in-game ads, product placement, dynamic in-game ads, advergames, game skinning, and sponsorships. Among these, static in-game ads and product placements are most popular. Static in-game advertising is kind of like boards as places to post ads, while produce placement, as an indirect advertising strategy, introduces real brand names in the buildings and cars used for games. Online game advertising has rapidly increased since 2000. When Nexon developed an online quiz game titled *Q Play*, the developer used some brands for the game's clothes and items, which was the first case of online game advertising. Later, Nexon advertised Coca Cola in its own car racing game *KartRider* as a form of product placement. NHN's *TailsRunner*, which is a running game, includes Nike as its major advertiser. Several major game developers, such as Neowiz and CJ Entertainment, also increase their revenues through different game advertising techniques. Several foreign and domestic manufacturers, such as Nike, Burger King, KFC, and SKT, have utilized product placement in online games to attract online game users and fans.

Although online game advertising is still limited to a few game genres, including sports and racing games (because, in the case of MMORPGs, advertising might hurt game users and fans' concentration), it is true to say that online game advertising is an emerging revenue source for corporations and advertising agencies. In fact, Korea's online game advertising market recorded $20 million in 2008, and it is expected to rise to $80 million in 2010 (Starbase 2008). Because 24.6% of people between the ages of 9 and 34 enjoy online games (the number for television is 23.5%), it is certain that advertisers and advertising agencies will target online gaming as a new advertising medium in the near future (Starbase 2008). The commodification of young game users and fans, whose demographic characteristics are similar, is evident. Because online game advertisers know the demographics of a specific target group through their registration information, advertisers easily find the best ads for those specific groups. Because young people frequently have access to their favorite online games by watching television game shows, watching game matches online, and by visiting online game stadiums where they enjoy games, online game advertising has already been considered one of the most effective advertising strategies.

As Dallas Smythe claimed in *Counterclockwise* (Smythe and Guback 1994), advertisers buy the services of audiences with predictable specifications who will pay attention in predictable numbers and at predictable times to particular means of communication (e.g., television, radio, newspapers, magazines, billboards, third-class mail, and now games).[6] As collectives, these audiences are commodities. As commodities, they are dealt with by producers and buyers (the latter being advertisers) (Smythe and Guback 1994; Artz 2008). Audiences are products that commercial networks sell to corporate advertisers. In the case of online gaming, game fans who are also game users are products that game developers, cable and IP television channels, and advertising agencies sell to corporate advertisers. Unlike the effect of television and movie stars on television audiences, however, online game teams, which are subsidiary companies of telecommunication and media corporations, directly change fans' user values to exchange values for profits.

As Henry Jenkins (2003, 2006) describes, active fans, as a specific type of audience, can be substantially distinguished from the majority of media consumers. For such fans, the act of watching a particular film or playing a certain video game can comprise an experiential unit that is interconnected to an expansive multitextual environment—one which may encompass magazines, books, collectibles, interactive media, online clubs, conferences, and role-playing events. As active participants, fans often appropriate corporate-generated imagery and then embellish or transform it with personal artistic expressions such as poetry, songs, paintings, scholarly essays, creative fiction, and digital films. Within the world of the Internet and online fan clubs, corporate products are treated as abstract digital bits of information, or, more concretely, as raw materials for fans' creative reinterpretation (Shefrin 2004). As Joost Raessens (2005, 383) points out, "participatory culture is a more active and productive attitude that makes special demands concerning the interpretation, the reconfiguration, and the construction of computer games." However, as Mark Andrejevic (2007, 137–138) rejects Jenkins' notion of participatory culture, calling some of Jenkins' earlier work on it "celebratory descriptions of fan activity" and "obverse" to his own treatment, the concept of participatory culture is controversial. In particular, when he wrote about reality television media, Andrejevic (2004) argued that cultural participation is always a commoditized activity: participation is the act of selling and buying. Online game fans are active and loyal to their favorite players and teams that are nevertheless part of big telecommunications and media corporations. Therefore, it is reasonable to say that the commodification process of online game fans is both a bottom-up fan-driven process and a top-down corporate-driven process. The commodification of online game fans is produced not only by game fans themselves but also by corporate strategies. Despite the fact that participation is symbolic and contextualized in meaning-making systems, ultimately, participation is also always commoditized (Pedersen 2008).

As many scholars claim, again, a crucial aspect of the transition from Fordism to post-Fordism has been the capitalist shift in emphasis from material to experiential goods, expanding markets for incessantly exhausted and renewed entertainment commodities that penetrate into every available space and moment of everyday life (cited by Kline, Dyer-Witheford, and de Peuter 2003). Online games can be seen as an example of this new regime of consumption (Kline, Dyer-Witheford, and de Peuter 2003, 183). In other words, "the audience was not simply passing time; it was also spending time in fairly regimented ways with advertising-supported media as the focus of attention (attention to a program), or as the focus of socializing" (going to a film together) (Meehan 1993, 382). Smythe (1977, 3) argued that leisure time, such as those hours of uncompensated labor in which the workers perform essential marketing functions for the producers of consumer goods, changes the relations between the production and reproduction of labor power.

The relationship between pro gamers and online game fans can be described in similar terms. The pro-gamers' participation in online game competition is commodified and marketed as both a paid-for leisure experience (through competition) and as a key selling point of corporations having game teams (Grimes 2006). More important, as Smythe (1981, 39–40) emphasized, audiences buy goods and spend their income accordingly. What makes the difference between general media audiences and online game audiences is that what online game audiences buy is often a special brand of consumer goods. Corporations owning online game teams clearly understand what they sell to the audience: not only goods and services but also their brands in the long run. Clearly, the most important thing for them is that audiences get used to the brand names of corporations that have game teams. Because fans or fan club members, as the audience of professional online gaming, are the first and major target consumers, which Smythe did not expect, the audience and audience commodity are created, as those corporations expected and planned (Grimes 2006, 987). During interviews of online gaming fans in 2007, one high school student who attended live matches twice a week, not only to learn strategy and see pro gamers she likes, but also to meet other enthusiasts, stated: "I switched my cellular phone to SKT as a symbol of my support to Choi who belongs to the SKT T1 team. Many fan club members identify themselves with pro gamers by purchasing goods and services provided by corporations who own pro teams" (Jin 1007, interview subject 5).

Along the lines of what Karl Marx (1867) argued, online game fans and the pro-gamers' world show precisely the process of commodification. Again, the relation between use-value and exchange-value is central to Marx's concept of commodity fetishism (Jhally 1987, 27). With their high-level game skills, pro gamers turn their use-value into exchange-value backed by corporations whose major goal is to make surplus through the commodification process. Likewise, online game fans have become valuable commodities by turning their use-value into exchange-value. Although online game fans are playful and joyful, these use-values ultimately become subordinate to exchange-value. As Grimes and Feenberg (2009, 108) point out, game play can now be evaluated in terms of the fixed criteria of strict formal rules in order to create a homogenous experience for every participant. That experience can then be commodified in accordance with broadcast rights, audience shares, and the demands of mass consumer culture. Online game teams' owners, who are usually telecommunications and media corporations, rapidly utilize online game fans and users as valuable commodities.

Summary

This chapter has been concerned with the commodification of online game fans (overall audiences), who are associated with the rapid growth of eSports. The process of commodification in online gaming is evident in the midst of the rapid growth of new media, because new media amplify the elements of Smythe's argument (Shimpach 2005). In addition to expanding the commodification of communication content, the recursive nature of digital systems expands the commodification of the entire communication process. Digital systems that measure and precisely monitor each information transaction are now used to refine the process of delivering audiences of viewers, listeners, readers, movie fans, and telephone and computer users to advertisers. In essence, companies can package (e.g., 17- to 25-year-old students in the case of online gaming) and repackage customers in forms that specifically reflect both their actual purchases and their demographic characteristics (Mosco 2009a). In Korea, children get used to the Internet at an early age, and nearly half of children between the ages of three and five use the Internet. Online games, where participants make friends and band together, have a strong appeal to Korean youth, who live in a tightly woven and hierarchical Confucian society. Under this circumstance, major corporations, especially from media and telecommunications industries, have utilized online game fans (who are also game users) to increase their revenues and corporate images. Online game fans, who are mainly in their teens and in their early twenties, are attractive and profitable commodities for many corporations, because they are currently major customers of new technologies. Online game fan club members are particularly loyal fans, and they have dedicated their time and energy to eSports as part of their daily lives. Although they are not wage workers, nor are they making money through their involvement in online gaming, they have turned themselves into valuable commodities.

Online game fans will continue to participate in their own commodification, consuming the brand images of professional game teams and corporations. Online games are often framed as sites of play and entertainment; however, their transformation into work platforms and the staggering amount of work that is being done through these games often goes unnoticed (Yee 2006a). As online gaming evolves in relation to a climate of corporate commodification, it seems likely that the pro-gamers' world will continue to produce the inevitable inequalities and insecurities. Of course, online game fans do work on advertising and program messages, but they have seldom worked in the form of wage labor. However, the real value produced by audiences, including online game fan club members, is economically relevant as long as the credibility of audience commodities and associated exploitation are seriously considered in the market. As the current debate operates primarily within the confines of the framework of commodification, both the players and online game fans can be seen as confirming the preeminence of exchange-value in online gaming.

III

Globalization and Game Empire

7

Adventure of Local Online Games toward Globalization

Introduction

The Korean online game industry has swiftly expanded its influence in the global cultural market as well as in the domestic market. With several successful online games, especially MMORPGs, Korea has penetrated numerous parts of the world, including Asia, North America, Latin America, Russia, and Europe. In 2007, the Korean online game market accounted for 46% of the entire Asia-Pacific market share, and Korean online games made up 32% of the world's online gaming market (Korea Game Industry Agency 2008). Although the market share of Korea's online games in Asia had decreased from 56% in 2005 to 46% in 2007 due to the increase in the Chinese online game industry, Korea's dominance in the global as well as Asian markets has continued to maintain its power (Kim, A. 2007). The online game industry is global, with game development companies in the United Kingdom (Argonaut, Climax, and Rare), Iceland (CCP), and Brazil (Ingis Games) (Consalvo 2006), but no other country has been as successful as Korea's online game industry.

The most popular online games made by Korean developers involve role-playing games (RPG) and casual games. In particular, *Lineage [I]* and *II*, two medieval fantasy MMORPGs released by Korean developer NCsoft in 1998 and 2003, respectively, have dominated the global online game market. They are available in Chinese, Japanese, English, and Korean language versions and possessed two of the largest commercial MMORPG communities before the emergence of *World of Warcraft*, developed by Blizzard Entertainment in the United States in 2005 (Mmogchart.com 2007), and *AION*, developed by NCsoft in 2008.

The rapid penetration of Korea's online games in the global game market has raised a fundamental question: will non-Western countries (currently Korea, but later perhaps China as well) be able to expand their cultural penetration, not only in the same region, but also in the global cultural market? It is also questionable whether this contra-flow in culture (i.e., a cultural flow from non-Western countries to Western countries) shows that an asymmetrical cultural flow exists in favor of the non-Western countries or that the United States' dominance has diminished. Using the *Lineage* games of NCsoft in conjunction with Korean online games as a case study, this chapter discusses the way in which the local online game industry has produced a global phenomenon. The goal of this chapter is to trace the production dynamics to identify the conditions that have rendered contra-flow in culture possible. It discusses the process by which a local culture is appropriated for the global audience in terms of hybridization in both content and marketing. The task this chapter sets out to accomplish is to understand the critical dialogue played by the global–local paradigm in "glocalizing" local culture for the global cultural market.

Primarily using a political economy approach and partially integrating it with a textual analysis, this chapter gives an overview of the supply side of the market for online games with a case study of *Lineage [I]* and *II*. By examining the Korean online game industry, this discussion illuminates some of the underexamined complexities inherent in the conception, development, implementation, and reception of online games in a global context.

Global–Local Paradigm in the Global Online Game Industry

The major frames of research in the process of the integration and interconnection of the global society, known as the phenomenon of globalization, have been who the major players are and which directions would be. Whether global cultural flow has been recognized as asymmetrical in favor of developed countries and which parts of society among the governments, transnational corporations, and local producers play a vital role in the globalization process are the most debatable subjects in the cultural globalization realm.

Several theoreticians, including Robert McChesney (1999, 2008), argue that TNCs—most of which are Western-based—have distributed their products to almost every corner of the world over the last several decades. Boyd-Barrett (2006) also points out that the U.S.-led Western media, both online and offline, and in various forms—information, infotainment, and entertainment—are global in their reach and influence. As Cees Hamelink (1983) states, the process of cultural homogenization is unprecedented in historical terms, and this process is closely connected to the spread of global capitalism. They claim globalization is a continuation of cultural imperialism whereby Western ideology is exported, destroying the diversity of local cultures and spreading a homogeneous global culture. While criticizing the role of TNCs in the global cultural flow, they tended to identify the West, and, in particular, the United States, as the center of a process of media-centric, capitalist cultural influence (Guback 1984; Schiller 1976; Nordenstreng and Varis 1974).

Several scholars dispute whether the global flow is necessarily a one-way flow, while conceding the predominance of Western media and cultural products in international communication (Sinclair and Harrison 2004; Tomlinson 1999; Giddens 1999). They argue that it is possible for cultural influence to flow from the periphery to the center and among peripheral nations.[1] From this perspective, global interconnectivity is not necessarily equal to global uniformity (Wu and Chan 2007). It is more a multidimensional and complex set of processes that allows the enrichment of global culture through diversity, as well as a variety of local discourses, codes, and practices (Featherstone 1990). As Iwabuchi (2002, 40) argues with the case of Japanese cultural penetration in Asia, and in particular in Taiwan,

the ascent of Japanese transnational cultural power should be considered in the global-local context, which attempts to attend simultaneously to the homogenizing forces of globalization and to transformative local practices in the formation of non-Western indigenized modernity, so as to understand the question of transnational cultural power.

In fact, several countries in Latin America, East Asia, and South Asia have developed unique cultural products and penetrated neighboring countries whose languages and cultures are similar. Mexico's Televisa, Brazil's Telenovela, and India's Bollywood have been examples of the success of local cultures confronting Western culture (Siriyuvasak and Shin 2007). Japanese animation, Korean films, and Arabic news have also witnessed a proliferation of multilingual and multifaceted growth, emanating from regional hubs of creative industries (Thussu 2006a, 180; 2006b).

As these cases prove, globalization of culture is a more complex connectivity, because the changing global entity under globalization should be considered in the global–local context. Local companies based in peripheral or semiperipheral countries are the natural candidates for globalizing local cultural products. Of course, not all local companies are well equipped for global marketing. Only those that understand the roles of global competition and posses other necessary cultural capital might have a chance of success. Incorporated into global capitalism, some local firms have not only gained experience of how to do business in the global market but have also become part of a global network involving both local and international players (Wu and Chan 2007, 199).

In recent years, some researchers have been attempting to add new evidence to this contra-flow in the case of video games, including console, handheld, online, and arcade games, because they are an intrinsic part of contemporary global flows of cultural goods, services, and images and because they have become part of a unique globalization process by providing the possibility of contra-flow (Kerr 2006a). In particular, Mia Consalvo (2006) made a unique case with Japanese console games, which have been considered examples of a growing non-Western presence throughout the world. Consalvo (2006, 120) argues that the video game industry is a hybrid encompassing a mixture of Eastern and Western businesses and (more importantly) cultures to a degree unseen in other media industries. Referring to New Zealand's online game *Beat Rugby*, Jay Scherer (2007, 476) also points out

the evolution of new media technologies and the increasingly sophisticated and interactive promotional operations of multinational corporations at the global–local nexus necessitate a critical examination of corporately-controlled electronic space of consumption.

Meanwhile, Cao and Downing (2008) argue that Korean and Chinese MMORPGs have also prevailed over popular global online games in East Asia and the West. As such, video games illustrate the ways in which games (both console and online games) are crucial to building global markets through a complex web of local franchises, regardless of the strong presence of popular Western products (Buckingham 2006, 4).

Due to the rapid growth of these cultural products in both Korean and regional markets, the possibility of contra-flow in video games has been gradually discussed. However, whether video games, and, in particular, online games, have penetrated the global market to a great degree remains controversial and yet much researched, because the successes of these countries' cultural products are arguably limited to the same region with a few exceptions. Although a few countries have increased their cultural dominance with online games, their global presence as cultural genres is still restricted. There is a huge gap between regional penetration and global presence, so the contra-flow has not yet fully taken place. In particular, as a reflection of its recent development and penetration, it is too early to confirm whether the contra-flow in the case of online games is authentic. This chapter contributes to this ongoing debate of the global–local paradigm with the case of rapidly growing Korean online games, including *Lineage [I]* and *II*.

From Local Online Games to Global Cultural Icons

Lineage [I] and *Lineage II* have a unique presence in the global cultural market, because the two games were developed in the periphery and exported on a large scale to Western countries. Unlike other cultural genres such as film, music, and television programming, which Western countries have dominated globally, the development of online games has been initiated in non-Western countries, particularly Korea. Headquartered in Seoul, Korea, NCsoft is home to the *Lineage* games, some of the world's most successful online RPGs. RPGs, in which players create or take on a character represented by various statistics, and which may include a developed persona, have had a relatively long history. The character's description may include specifics, such as species, race, gender, and occupation, and may also include various abilities, such as strength and dexterity, usually represented numerically (Wolf 2002, 130). Of course, there were several RPG video games, such as *Anvil of Dawn, Dragon Lore 2, Mageslayer, Phantasy Star* (from *Dungeons and*

Dragons), and the *Ultima* series. However, *Lineage* games, as online versions of the RPG genre, have become some of the most successful RPG games developed by a Korean game industry (Wolf 2002). These RPGs are no more than online remakes of these early video games due to their unique characteristics and texts.

When NCsoft launched Korean service for its flagship product, *Lineage [I]* in 1998, only 17 players were connected to the game, although online games in Korea boomed as the American-developed game *Star-Craft* made its way into the local market in 1998. According to game producer Blizzard Entertainment, it sold 2.8 million copies in Korea, almost half its global sales as of October 2003 (You 2003). *StarCraft's* popularity was soon overtaken by *Lineage*, but *StarCraft* remains one of the most popular games in Korea. *Lineage* had been the biggest online game in the world, and NCsoft ranks as one of the world's leading MMORPG developers.[2] In 1997, the company, still in its early stages, posted sales of $436,000; in 2002, sales soared to $46 million (You 2003). As of early 2007, *Lineage [I]* had more than 4.3 million subscribers and simultaneous connections in the hundreds of thousands worldwide with revenues of $112.4 million. *Lineage [I]* became particularly popular in Asia, but later was played worldwide. When *Lineage* was launched in Taiwan in 2000, sales of the game reached $1.4 million in only two months and attracted 200,000 subscribers (*Korea Herald* 2000). As a tangible reflection of its penetration worldwide, NCsoft has created branch offices in nine countries, including Taiwan, Japan, China, and North America, and it has signed a publishing contract with several countries, including with Digital Legend Entertainment in Spain and Spacetime Studios in the United States. Meanwhile, launched in 2003, *Lineage II* continues the game series' hugely popular status with 110,000 simultaneous connections and 2 million memberships in Korea, as well as successful launches in other territories worldwide (NCsoft 2007a). It had a worldwide subscriber base of 14 million as of February 2007 (*Korea Times* 2007), and its worldwide revenue was as much as $147.2 million in 2008 (NCsoft 2009b).

There are several significant differences between *Lineage [I]* and *II*, and one of the major characteristics of *Lineage II* in production is the development process, because *Lineage II* changed the concept of the online game industry by ushering in the blockbusterization of Korean online games. Only a few years ago, game development was often characterized as the ultimate cottage industry for the information age (*Economist* 1997, 175; Kline, Dyer-Witheford, and de Peuter 2003). This view is losing its validity due to massive capital investment and the expansion of employees. In fact, the cost of the development of one game in Korea was only $180,000 in 1999. With *Lineage II*, the cost has soared. NCsoft spent as much as $8 million on the development of *Lineage II*, and 70 developers spent three years to develop the game (Ji 2003). The company has also spent about $20 million for marketing. Since then, Korea's online game developers have begun to make blockbuster-level games, and the cost of developing one game has soared.

With these two consecutive successes, NCsoft became one of the largest online game developers and publishers. In Korea, its employees number more than 1,200, compared to only 20 on average in other Korean game companies. The *Lineage* games also generated as much as $1.55 billion in revenues between 1998 and 2006; out of this, 30% was from abroad (Kwon 2007). When NCsoft recorded $338 million in revenues in 2006, for example, 46% of revenues came from foreign countries, including 20% from the United States and 12% from Europe (NCsoft 2009b). The *Lineage* games are two of the largest cultural goods produced by a Korean firm to make such massive revenue in such a short period of time, dominating the global market. The *Lineage* games, originated and developed in a non-Western region, are some of the most popular cultural genres in the Korean game sector, and they are seemingly interconnected with the global cultural market.

Cultural Hybridization in Local Online Games

There are several key elements that are considered contributing factors to the rapid growth of Korea's online game industry and to its global presence, such as cultural authenticity, hybridization of the text, high levels of new technology, and fantastic storytelling of games like *Lineage*. Several online games, including *The Kingdom of Winds*—the world's first graphic massively multiplayer online game—originally depended on cartoons. *Lineage* is also based on Shin Il-sook's fantasy cartoons, and it is thought by many consumers to be one of the most interesting online games, one that clearly understands the nature of Koreans

(Kim, J. I. 2005). Launched in September 1998, *Lineage [I]* is an RPG in which players can choose to take on characters from four different classes (knight, prince, elf and dark elf, or wizard), developing these characters individually or banding together to form hunting parties and pledges, battling medieval fantasy monsters and even each other. Each class provides different experiences and levels of challenge. *Lineage* is a network game in which players wage battle in a cyberworld set in medieval times with weapons such as swords, shields, and magical rings that enable users to change their identities.

Although the game drew from medieval Europe for its content, it is integrated with Korean nature. The game enables complex interaction among its players coupled with the game's massive scale. The game can be played alone, but its allure is that it is community-based, which has been an important feature for Korean online gamers, and likewise for East Asian users. *Lineage*'s developer and publisher (NCsoft) claims that players have more fun by joining hunting parties and forming allegiances, heightening their abilities to fight foes and monsters. This gives gamers the sense of a common goal and the chance to socialize with other players (You 2003). As discussed in chapter 2, the mass play culture of Koreans, especially young people, has become one of the major contributing factors for the growth of online gaming, because they like to play with friends (clans and/or guilds in games), and NCsoft utilized this aspect of Korean culture in producing *Lineage [I]*.

Because it is set in the Kingdom of Aden in medieval Europe, and the game's objective is to overthrow the evil, illegitimate king, the basic storyline is Western. However, the Korean developer integrated Western game storylines with Korean cultural settings. NCsoft appealed to Korean values, which emphasize solidarity, affiliation, and family matters (Kim, J.I. 2005). NCsoft realized that Korean online gamers like player versus player (PvP) games, characterized by graceful movements and community interactions, and they encourage role players to take roles within a social hierarchy and engage in coordinated strategies or other collective activity, while U.S. players like PvE (player versus environment, including computer) games (Park, M. 2008; Martinsons 2005). Usually the PvE mode can be played alone, and often this involves battling computer-controlled artificial intelligence creatures or solving a riddle, as in console games, which is different from PvP games.

In *Lineage [I]*, the remaining members of the royal family, represented by the prince class, form groups called Blood Pledges with the aim of returning the throne to its rightful lineage. Blood Pledges, which are similar to guilds, allow the members of the group to share their magic, a pledge-only messaging system, and a common house. In addition, each character is able to experience collaboration, competition, and war while involved in a Blood Pledge. *Lineage*'s popularity is based on innovative hybridization—a mix of a global RPG story line with local mentality—of the online game. As several scholars have noted, hybridity describes mixed genres and identities (Kolar-Panov 1996; Tufte 1995; Consalvo 2006). In particular, the game industry itself is a hybrid encompassing a mixture of Western culture and non-Western cultures to a degree unseen in other media industries. This kind of achievement by a non-Western corporation is indicative of the hybridization of the digital games industry.

Lineage II utilizes more subtle production strategies. For *Lineage II*, NCsoft employed the same setting and basic gameplay as the original *Lineage*, but it added new features to the MMORPG genre, such as three-dimensional graphics that enhance the player's experience in an immersive environment. *Lineage II* focuses on combat and player-versus-player battles. Game players can create their own characters from five races, most being in either fighter or mystic classes: Human, Elf, Dark Elf, Orc, and Dwarf. Then, game players go one-on-one against other players or become a member of a clan that takes on entire armies of opposing players. The battles of *Lineage II* are realistic.

Lineage II also emphasizes Korean and overall East Asian characteristics. In the game, friendships strengthen and tensions become frayed among players who adopt alliances between clans and organized party systems. Furthermore, the big online games wave enables and encourages people to communicate and further interact with each other. Through games and related activities, a new generation of online gamers form friendships, enjoy chatting and blogging, and even create their own communities, which are representations of Korean cultural traditions. By appealing to major Korean mentalities, such as solidarity and affiliation, *Lineage* games have achieved huge success among Korean game players, as well as among other East Asian users.

What is even more remarkable in *Lineage* games is that the achievement in quantitative terms is in fact cultural creativity. Many experts agree that Korean online games have marked an important change in the human art of storytelling. Espen Aarseth, a world pioneering theorist in video game theory once concluded about the Korean multiplayer game *Lineage*: "These games are not only the future of gaming, they are huge social experiments that will affect and shape the future of human communication" (Yi 2006). These Korean online games create stories in a new narrative paradigm different from any art of storytelling that existed in human history. They are unique stories in which a user becomes cognizant of the values of social justice and human freedom by creating a conflict that lasts for over 1,000 hours that enables him/her to actively take part in it as a protagonist (Yi 2006).

In addition, one of the major traits of *Lineage* games is the simple interface, which allows people of all ages and genders to easily and quickly begin playing and enjoying the game. New content in the form of "episodes" keep the game fresh. Each episode reflects feedback from the community and the work of dedicated development teams within NCsoft to support *Lineage*'s immense player base. NCsoft also has 250 game masters who deal with complaints from gamers, while providing ideas and opinions of users to the requisite product development and enhancement teams (Kim, M. H. 2005). As one of the major examples of participatory media, interactivity is a key in the growth of online games. Gamers are able to control the game's proceedings and/or its conclusion. In contrast to a passive film audience, an interactive game player is able to take up the role of narrator and influence the course of events and actions, possibly as a character in the plot (Raessens 2005).

NCsoft has utilized this characteristic of online games coupled with the Korean mentality in the process of developing and updating *Lineage* games. The popularity of *Lineage* games depends on their sophistication, using cultural authenticity rooted in Korean society, which has resulted in at least part of the globalization strategies of the *Lineage* games. The developers are faithful to the local culture and maintain a sense of cultural authenticity, which paradoxically results in success not only in the local market but also in the global market. Along with its (g)localization strategies, discussed in the next section, their sophistication in using national cultural authenticity has become one of the most significant parts of the *Lineage* games' global penetration.

(G)localization Strategies of the Non-Western Game Industry

Compared to *Lineage [I]*, which emphasized Korean cultural character-istics and hybridization, the overseas success of *Lineage II* comes from its localization strategy, which has elsewhere been the strategic business model of global media giants, including Disney and Viacom. These global media corporations prioritize gaining insider status within regional and local markets as they operate around the world (Consalvo 2006). However, now the local game industry has adopted the localization process of non-Western culture in Western societies. Adopting the popular major media firm's slogan, "think globally, act locally," which is a business motto of Viacom and Disney (Fung 2006), NCsoft has initi-ated glocalization for its gaming business, opening branches in Western countries, developing games with Western publishers in these local (Western) areas, and developing a new global financing model.

To begin with, NCsoft acknowledges a globalization trend by adapt-ing to the user's local taste. Unlike other Korean and foreign game developers and publishers who sell the rights of games to foreign com-panies, NCsoft's strategies are conceived and marketed through actual local needs and expectations. Aiming to become a global game company, NCsoft has established branches and/or joint ventures in several coun-tries, including Japan, China, Taiwan, Thailand, Europe, and the United States. The number of employees in these branches is about 1,300, similar to that of NCsoft in Korea (1,259) (NCsoft 2007b). NCsoft has pursued "a global infrastructure, local content strategy" to intensify the global infrastructure by developing localized content, because it believes that gaming is culture that should fit local taste (Bu 2007).

NCsoft has been rapidly expanding its reach in Asia. In 2000, NCsoft created a joint-venture company, NC Gamania, with Gamania of Hong Kong. It also established the joint-venture company NC Japan with the Softbank Group of Japan in 2001. The company established the joint-venture company NC-Sina with SINA.com, in China in 2003, and released *Lineage* service Tian Tang (meaning Heaven) as a service name for China, which is being touted as the biggest online game market (Yang 2003). The firm also established NCsoft Japan and NCsoft China in 2006.

NCsoft has drastically expanded its market beyond Korea and neighboring countries. Under its ambition to globalize, the company looked at U.S. and European markets. *Lineage*'s penetration into China and Taiwan has been particularly successful due in part to cultural similarities; it will not be so easy for them to crack the U.S. and European gaming markets (Song 2004). NCsoft recognized that the international arena would not be easy to penetrate—not because of a technological gap but because of significant legal and cultural differences.

In order to penetrate the Western game market, NCsoft first opened NC Interactive in Austin, Texas, United States, in 2000, and signed Richard Garriott, the U.S. game programmer best known for *ULTIMA Online*, and 19 others from Destination Games Inc. in Austin. NCsoft paid Destination $33.4 million in stock and cash for *Tabula Rasa*, the next-generation Internet game being developed by Garriott's team (NCsoft 2007a). NC Interactive, as the North American arm of NCsoft, focuses on operations, marketing, localization, and third-party publishing (NCsoft 2007b). In a bid to tap into these lucrative markets, NCsoft also acquired an American company, ArenaNet of Seattle, Washington, which consists of the core developing members of *StarCraft* and *WarCraft*, in 2002. NCsoft has four development studios and one subsidiary company in the United States.

In addition, NCsoft established NC Europe Ltd., in London, United Kingdom, in 2004, to provide entertainment services on the Internet, such as online game publishing in Europe. It also launched its service for *Lineage II* that same year in Europe. Because American-made online games were dominating the game industry in Europe, Korean-made games did not make significant strides in Europe until recent years. Through publishing contracts with several firms throughout the world, such as Digital Legend Entertainment in Spain and Spacetime Studios in the United States in 2006, NCsoft has extensively penetrated the global game market, from Asia to North America and Europe. Unlike products in other cultural genres, such as film, music, and television programming, where Western countries dominate or initiate localization processes, *Lineage* games have expanded their local presence, making themselves a true global genre developed in a non-Western country through localization strategies taking place in several Western countries.

As discussed, a few cultural genres, such as films and television programs, have made a local presence tantamount to globalization in the same region by exporting a limited number of cultural products. Most of the newly abundant commercial cultural products have no inclination to cut free of prevailing property relations or the existing interstate system but aim instead to carve out a lucrative niche within their sphere of influence (Schiller 2007). However, the emergence of the *Lineage* games in the global market has somewhat changed this contemporary concept of localization by targeting and successfully penetrating not only regional but also Western countries.

Second, NCsoft's most significant local strategy has been the development of *Lineage II* in the United States, not in Korea. *Lineage II* was planned as a global product from the first phase of production, and it was mainly developed at the company's California design lab (Cho 2005a). During the development process, NCsoft named Adam Davidson, who previously worked for Rockstar Games and Acclaim Entertainment, the North American producer for *Lineage II*. Davidson and the *Lineage II* team in North America were headquartered in Austin, Texas, where Richard Garriott worked as CEO and Davidson served as associated producer of the game, hoping to guide the game's launch as well as the successful implementation of three major game expansions (Barriault 2005). Davidson argues that NCsoft's North American branches work not only as developers but also as testers on *Lineage II* and its expansions in terms of the effects of special items. He emphasizes that the game was originally designed for the Asian gaming market but it has evolved to suit the style of play of the North American market (Lafferty 2007):

The fifth expansion, for example, increased "soloability" for Americans. We've continued to work towards making the early gameplay experience one that caters to a variety of play-styles, not solely those preferred in Asia. By making it faster and easier to progress through the early stages of the game, we hope to usher players through the learning phases and into the meat-and-potatoes of the product, the high-end game, in a more reasonable timeframe.

As discussed, most Asian players enjoy PvP games while U.S. players prefer PvE games, the latter of which have emphasized individual game play. In order to attract American users, the company has localized its original game by adopting American game styles. While *Lineage [I]* utilizes its cultural heritage from the Confucian hierarchy (working together as a team), *Lineage II* adopts what American game users want (to be a hero-king Lone Ranger). As Barry Ip (2008, 216) argues, the user experience is proportionately linked to increased functionality in *Lineage* games. NCsoft's other games have chosen the same strategy. Games such as *Guild Wars* (which was developed at ArenaNet, another American-based developing studio owned by NCsoft in 2002) and *City of Heroes* were also made in the United States to meet the expectations of American gamers; the latter is not available in Korea (Cho 2005a).

In this regard, Castells (2001) points out that TNCs are no longer offering visual spectacles to seduce target markets and differentiate brands; instead, contemporary post-Fordist marketing strategies are encouraging local audiences to engage the cybernetic spectacle and create their own personalized relationships with commodity signs. As Jay Scherer (2007, 475) claims, the game and electronics community facilitated a range of consumption process for a transnational audience, which means that the online game company makes the game as accessible as possible for a global audience. NCsoft, as a non-Western-based online TNC, has strategically employed the localization process to attract local audiences; in this case, American audiences. As Aphra Kerr (2006a) points out, only a small number of large companies are involved in the development, publishing, and distribution of the most successful MMORPGs, and by adapting globalization strategies, NCsoft has penetrated Western game markets with their *Lineage* games.

Finally, *Lineage II* introduced a new global form for the financial structure of the game, which is another configuration of the globalization strategy. Until 2003, the online game norm in terms of the financial structure was that subscribers paid a monthly fee to play. For *Lineage [I]*, players paid a monthly fee and downloaded the software. However, *Lineage II* introduced sixty-day game time cards for a suggested retail price of $29.99, as well as a monthly subscription format. Several games have followed this financial structure. For example, *Guild Wars*, developed by ArenaNet, used the same format, and it cost approximately $50 for the basic version; the company released an expansion pack every six months instead of charging for a subscription (Colbourne 2005).

Of course, due to the necessity to quickly penetrate the global market, NCsoft has adopted licensed service like many online game firms in recent years. The company has negotiated a deal with the Asian Media Development Group, the largest distributor of computer games in the Philippines, for the licensed service of *Lineage II* in the Philippines, Singapore, and Malaysia. Because NCsoft has provided game service in foreign countries through local subsidiaries, the agreement with the Asian Media Development Group represents the first licensing contract for the game, valued at $5.5 million (*Korea Times* 2007). The hybridization of *Lineage II* in a form of glocalization, which is a strategic mix of non-Western brands with Western developing and marketing processes, has greatly contributed to the development of the Korean online game industry. As Iwabuchi (2002) argues, countries and regions with shared cultural connections develop regional geocultural markets, where dynamic intraregional media flows are generated. The active intraregional flow of online games between China, Korea, and Taiwan suggests a geocultural market paradigm (Cao and Downing 2008, 519). However, as the case of the *Lineage* games proves, local online games go beyond regional markets representing intraregional cultural flows. *Lineage* games have expanded their rate of penetration in the United States (for example, from 15.7% in 2005 to 19.9% in 2006 as foreign exports) and Europe, and they are a part of contra-flow, as in the case of films and television programs.

NCsoft's localization strategy in production has also greatly influenced other online game developers who want to expand abroad. For example, Hangame Japan, the online game portal introduced by Korea's NHN, used a localization approach. Hangame Japan approached the Japanese game market, holy ground to console platforms, such as the Sony PlayStation and Nintendo series, beyond something of a hybrid of Korean and Japanese culture. Instead, NHN Japan used a localization strategy and did not hesitate to claim it as a Japanese firm in terms of its organization. Among some 320 employees, only 50 are Korean nationals. The manager positions are filled with local people as well. It was important to do so because Japanese gamers have different tastes than Koreans. Chun Yang Hyun, CEO of the company, states; "in Japan, people don't want to play games to compete with each other. They want to be together with others through games. They like games in which they can make friends, not foes" (Cho 2007a). With the localization strategy, the peak-time user count has rapidly increased, from about 2,000 in

2001 to 120,000 in January 2007. NHN also established NHN USA in Mountain View, California, in the heart of Silicon Valley, because the company was to become a major player worldwide, and getting a foothold in the United States was an important step for NHN (Ramstad 2006, D10).

Korea's most popular online games, involving role-playing sagas and casual games, have rapidly penetrated other countries. As discussed in chapter 3, several casual online games, including *Pangya*, *Wyd*, and *Groove Party*, have been well received in many countries, alongside several famous MMORPGs. Beginning with the *Lineage* games, Korea's online game companies have greatly expanded their global presence and have made Korea a powerhouse in the online game genre worldwide. The Korean game industry has connected the global game market through the contra-flow of the new cultural genre in the twenty-first century. While several competitors, especially Chinese game firms, have emerged in the game market, the Korean online game industry currently dominates the global market, and Korean online games are expected to continue their hegemony in the near future. The local game company has rapidly utilized globalization strategies that Western media giants sought. As locally based game enterprises, NCsoft and several Korean game firms have driven glocalization to adapt to local cultures (in this case, many Western countries), and to link up with local partners, again Western game companies, in order to sustain their expansion. As several U.S. media giants have adopted a strategy known as "think globally, act locally" to expand their dominance globally, now local game firms also utilize glocalization as a business strategy to penetrate other parts of the world effectively.

Summary

This chapter has discussed whether non-Western countries are able to expand their cultural penetration, not only in the same region but also in the global cultural market with the case of online games. The analysis has demonstrated the presence of the glocalization paradigm, through hybridization of Korean online games in the global market. In this analysis, Korean online gaming as a genre has shown a unique contra-flow, or it could be said that *Lineage* games have opened the possibility of contra-flow in the online game sector. *Lineage* games have experienced a dramatic growth rate, gaining popularity and blazing trails in the development of business models over the past several years. Korea has promoted online games as a major part of the digital economy, and Korea has become a major power in today's world of digital technology, succeeding in the commercialization of online games globally (Jin and Chee 2008).

As the case of the *Lineage* games proves, online gaming has made globalization from the semiperiphery possible and has initiated a new era in the global cultural market. Online games allow people from all over the world to interact with each other. The globalization of Korea's game products (and, in particular, online games) rapidly bridges the gap between the global and local through strategic alliances formed between firms and individuals, which has resulted in creating a global virtual community. Several core countries, in particular, the United States and Japan, have dominated the console market, and, therefore, it is controversial whether the Japanese console game industry is a good case of contra-flow; in the case of online gaming, the Korean game industry contemporarily becomes a case of contra-flow.[3] Online gaming is promoting a non-Western capitalist global society, and online gaming is a new medium to promote non-Western culture to the world. As Aphra Kerr (2006b) points out, online games must attend to local cultural practices, tastes, and social structures if they are to succeed across the major markets, and the *Lineage* games have delicately utilized this business norm to penetrate not only Asian markets but also Western markets. Local media texts have embodied global consumer culture and played a full-fledged role in propagating it, and then have turned themselves into transnational products (Lee 2004).

What *Lineage* demonstrates is that the local cultures of developing countries can be made popular around the world. NCsoft, as a Korean-based TNC, is found to be the primary mover of the project (Kerr and Flynn 2003). Developing countries must overcome the lack of resources and face global competition from Western-based TNCs, as well as the marketing obstacles set by foreign markets. To meet these challenges, NCsoft and several Korean online game companies negotiated for globalization through the hybridization of content and marketing. The alliances with other organizations, such as TNCs and local companies in other countries, can help to solve the problems by pooling resources, competencies, and skills. Culture flows to survive, and as it flows, it shifts, warps, changes, and modifies, to become hybridized, strange, and new (Consalvo 2006). In its production of online games, NCsoft proves that local producers must maintain a global–local perspective, exploiting the distinctive local culture on the one hand and universalizing it for the world on the other (Wu and Chan 2007, 212).

Although the success of *Lineage* alone cannot spell the end of the cultural dominance of Western countries, it represents an anomaly to be reckoned with. It at least demonstrates the possibility and a way in which a local culture can be globalized on a significant scale. The success of the *Lineage* games lends support to the argument that globalization is not necessarily directed from the West, and that it is instead a multi-directional and multidimensional process. The globalization of local cultures is a dynamic process that needs to be constantly monitored. Unlike other cultural genres, video games, including console and online games, were pioneered and dominated by non-Western companies from the beginning, and this trend will be continued and intensified with the entrance of Chinese online games into the global market.

There are cautionary remarks that need to be made. The apparent flourishing of online game capital in Korea is precarious. Despite experiencing dramatic growth over the last decade, the online game industry is now in a phase of stagnation, due to increasing competition inside and out. Several major online game companies are already experiencing eroding growth. *Lineage* has experienced a shrinking share in the global role-playing market due to the rapid growth of rival title *World of Warcraft*. Until 2005, the combined share of the original *Lineage* and three-dimensional-based *Lineage II* stood at 45%, followed by *World of Warcraft* (22%) in the global online game market. However, *World of Warcraft* took a 52.9% share in June 2006, outpacing NCsoft, which held 22.4% (Lee 2006a, 17). Technologies offer potential opportunities as well as threats (Preston and Kerr 2001). In particular, there is a danger that TNCs may finally take control of local cultural resources once they recognize their value (Schiller 2007). Most of all, hybridization is not merely the mixing, blending, and synthesizing of different elements that ultimately form a culturally faceless whole. In the course of hybridization, cultures often generate new forms and make new connections with one another (Wang and Yeh 2005; Ryoo 2009). Although the *Lineage* games have successfully established a new form of culture by mixing Western stories and Korean characteristics, only a limited number of Korean games follow this trend. One must use caution when looking for trends of the successful hybridization of online games produced by Korean game firms targeting the global market.

The *Lineage* games have changed the norm of globalization and have greatly influenced the future course of how local culture will flow amid globalization. However, the challenge of the local cultural industry is to maintain and/or expand its global presence with the continuing development of new games, as well as sophisticating its glocalization and/or hybridization strategies.

8

From the Cottage Industry to Transnational Media Giants

Introduction

Over the last ten years, online gaming has grown rapidly and become one of the most popular activities in the global cultural market. Since the early 1970s, when Nolan Bushnell started Atari with two fellow engineers, ever-increasing numbers of entrepreneurs have invested in the emerging new medium, which has resulted in the exponential growth of the online game industry. Until the late twentieth century, the online game industry was often characterized as the ultimate cottage industry for the information age (*Economist* 1997, 175). Post-Fordism is the era of small high-tech companies, and new digital production provides tangible advantages to small nimble firms that can swiftly adapt to changing technologies and market conditions (Kline, Dyer-Witheford, and de Peuter 2003, 170). With fewer than 20 employees per company on average and limited funds available for the development of new games (software), game developers were very much like small stores through the end of the twentieth century.

In recent years, the concept of online gaming as the ultimate cottage industry has lost its accuracy due to increasing ownership of the online game industry by a few large corporations, such as Vivendi, Sony, and Microsoft (Jin and Chee 2008). Individual investors, venture capitalists, and media giants have rapidly become part of the emerging new media (Kline, Dyer-Witheford, and de Peuter 2003, 177); the online game industry has been one of the most profitable sectors in several Asian countries, including Korea and China.

The online game industry has been swiftly transnationalized. Ever since French conglomerate Vivendi, one of the largest media and entertainment corporations in the world, purchased Blizzard Entertainment —a computer game developer and publisher headquartered in the United States—in 1998, the online game industry has been the acquisition target of large media and telecommunications corporations, as well as computer firms in Western and non-Western countries. In large part, this is because the online game industry is a symbol of digital technology and its integration with youth culture. Several global media and computer corporations, including IBM, Philips, and Disney, have expanded their roles in the game sector globally, and several local-based TNCs, including Shanda in China and SK Telecom and Samsung in Korea, have become involved in this booming digital economy and culture. These TNCs became global megamedia giants by acquiring smaller developers and publishers. Digital entertainment can evolve from the blossoming of the small-scale high-tech industry amidst post-Fordism, as the expanding power of media conglomerates unequivocally demonstrates (Kline, Dyer-Witheford, and de Peuter 2003, 171). The online game industry has been a battleground among major TNCs seeking global leader status in the dynamic, high-margin game world.

The online game industry has adopted commercial strategies similar to those of the Hollywood movie industry, the cultural industry perhaps most closely associated with the process of globalization for the past 80 years. Major online game companies have expanded on a global scale, vertically and horizontally integrating through capital investments, alliances, and takeovers, as they seek to control platforms, content development, publishing, and distribution (Kerr and Flynn 2003). More importantly, many online game firms have transnationalized through the exchange of people, new business models, and financing systems.

Very few scholarly works have been written that explain the recent transnationalization of the online game industry and how these changes have transformed the industry. This chapter examines the structural transnationalization of the online game industry, recent trends of TNCs, and their engagement in the online game industry to ascertain whether these trends are confirmation that TNCs play pivotal roles in the cultural market. The focus is on capital flow, people and financing, and the ways in which the online game industry has developed its transnationalization process, in order to fully understand the nature of transnationalization. The chapter also explores whether emerging online game firms, as part of the new cultural industry in non-Western countries, in particular Korea and China, have changed the traditional form of the global flow of cultural products and capital—from Western countries to non-Western countries—by blurring the dichotomy of the West and the East. In other words, it discusses whether the transnationalization of the online game industry has promoted a shift of traditional interpretations of cultural dominance by Western countries in the global market in the midst of globalization.

Transnationalization and Globalization of Digital Economy and Culture

Since the mid-1980s, the media and cultural industries in several regions have experienced significant transnationalization, an economic/cultural phenomenon. Several previous studies isolated the economic perspective from the cultural viewpoint by concentrating on the financing of the cultural industry (the act that initiates the cycle of production, distribution, and exhibition) (Wasser 1995). The transnationalization of industry refers to the development of the production relations and work processes among productive units located in different countries (Mato 2005). The transnational process is not limited to production, which means transnationalization and globalization as phenomena produce a state of culture in transnational motion—flows of people, trade, communication, ideas, technologies, finance, social movements, cross-border movement, and more (Shome and Hedge 2002, 174). As Preben Sepstrup (1990) points out, it is crucial to understand transnationalization as a more complex process, because the international flow of the production, supply, and consumption of these messages in turn further affects the production and reproduction of culture and ideology.

Transnationalization in the cultural industry started in the beginning of the postwar era when Hollywood invaded Western European countries and later Asian countries—traditionally the two largest export markets for U.S. films. While governments had renewed earlier attempts to protect national cultural space by imposing restrictions on the deluge of Hollywood exports for diverse reasons and with considerable variation, Hollywood outflanked them by turning to coproductions and foreign direct investment (Guback 1969). As Herbert Schiller (1976) pointed out, the dominance of the United States and a few European nations in the global flow of media products has become an integral component of Western imperialism, and the powerful U.S. communication industry particularly forced global commercialization on the international communication system.

In recent years, with the development of the Internet from its usage in the military to a worldwide audience of 1.4 billion users as of June 2008, the rise of communication technology has brought globalization and transnationalization to a whole new level (Internet World Stats 2008). Although transnationalization happens in every sector in media and culture, starting with Hollywood and later the broadcasting and music industries, transnationalization has rapidly developed with the growth of new technologies in the twenty-first century. As Boyd-Barrett (2006) argues, transnationalization has been especially phenomenal in knowledge-based industries, such as the Internet, broadband, satellite, online gaming, and telecommunications, strongly represented among TNCs. Transnationalization is a phenomenon that is flourishing, and, with the development of technologies in the information and communication sectors of the global economy, a fusion between the East and the West is becoming visible in many aspects of life.

What makes ICT transnationalization different from that of the old media, such as film and broadcasting, is the role of TNCs of non-Western countries. In traditional media sectors, Western, particularly U.S.-based TNCs, have played a key role, because they have had capital, skills, and a workforce dominating the global media industry, based on their advanced economies and technology and culture. ICT industries, such as the Internet, broadband, and mobile technologies, on the other hand, have become battlegrounds between the United States and non-Western regions. Asian-based TNCs, including Sony, Samsung, and LG, have especially challenged the continuation of U.S. hegemony in the ICT industries.

Against this backdrop, transnationalization in the online gaming industry should be examined from a variety of angles, from business to cultural aspects of companies and people across the globe. The global impacts of the online gaming industry, from a business standpoint, show companies from the East or the West trying to broaden their markets from a domestically exclusive market niche to a worldwide audience to increase revenue and power in the gaming world. Other forms of transnationalization of the industry include global online gaming job opportunities, as well as hundreds of choices of games, including both Western- and Eastern-originated games. This blend of the East and the West has combined the two major markets into one in which gaming companies are now targeting potentially billions of users.

A transnational media order is coming into being that is remapping media spaces and involving new media practices, flows, and products (Chalaby 2007). Arguably, an international reach is no longer exclusive to Western-based conglomerates, as an increasing number of smaller media companies from the developing world are expanding overseas (Thussu 2006). In the corporate world, media conglomerates are adopting a new organizational structure and management mentality, mutating from local to transnational media companies (Barlett and Ghoshal 1998). Headquarters give affiliates growing autonomy and categorize them according to their strengths and resources and then line them up into an interdependent corporate network. This new organizational structure enables these companies to combine global efficiency with responsiveness to local and regional markets (Chalaby 2007). The online game industry as a latecomer in the cultural market has not only further deepened the convergence between computing, telecommunications, and electronic media, but has also developed the integration between the text and the hardware through its transnationalization process. This chapter sheds some light on the ongoing debate on transnationalization and globalization.

Transnationalization of Online Game Businesses and Industries

The online game industry has become one of the most significant sectors of the global cultural industry due to the vast number of game users and large revenues over the last ten years. In particular, Asian online game markets, including Korea and China, showed the fastest growth and accounted for half of the online gaming revenue in 2006 (PriceWater-HouseCoopers 2007). Also, as of July 2007, the worldwide online gaming population reached 217 million people (ComScore 2007). The online game center is located in Asia, and Korea and China are two megaplayers in the region. Japan has lagged behind these countries in the online game area, with most Japanese preferring console and hand-held games (PriceWaterHouseCoopers 2007). These astounding numbers, the potential for online gaming in Asia, and the increase in revenues worldwide is convincing companies from the West to invest in or purchase businesses in the East. With the capabilities of broadband, a single dominant online game can attract gamers from across the globe. In addition, Asia has tremendous potential based on the huge population centers of China and India.

In particular, what the online game industry makes unique is that two major forces, Western and Asian corporations, have worked together, which has resulted in the rapid transnationalization of the market. In several cultural sectors, such as film and broadcasting, Western countries and corporations have dominated, while a few countries, including Brazil, Mexico, and Korea, have arguably emerged as local-based transnational cultural players for niche markets. However, in the online game industry, Asia-based corporations sometimes compete with Western-based corporations and, at other times, cooperate with them to develop programs and to attract game players throughout the world. In this chapter, the transnationalization of both Asian and Western game industries are documented and the major causes for the transnationalization of the industry are analyzed.

Transnationalization of Asian Online Game Industries

Transnational game corporations have rushed into the Korean game market by setting up subsidiaries and by establishing a form of joint venture with Korean game developers and publishers. Major corporations from the West, such as EA, Blizzard Entertainment, Microsoft, UbiSoft, and Intel, are urgently establishing their markets in the East, with company buyouts and mergers to strengthen their global hold on the online gaming industry. As a reflection of the swift growth of Asian online game markets, foreign-based TNCs have rapidly entered Asia. In particular, Western publishers have been taking on other functions in the production and distribution cycle of the Asian markets. Publishers have been acquiring distribution channels in order to ensure that their products reach retailers, and they have been buying into or taking over development studios (Kerr 2006b, 51). This increasing vertical integration suggests that, over time, a situation may emerge in which a small number of publishers dominate the industry, as the major studios do in the film industry (Kerr 2006b).

In fact, EA, the world's biggest video game publisher, recently purchased 15% of a Chinese online gaming operator to enlarge its control in Asia. EA paid about $167 million to The9 Ltd to pursue its strategy of partnering with a proven regional operator to provide online games to Asia. EA has already dominated the Western market, but with 41 million online gamers and a total spending of 6.54 billion Yuan in 2006, China has been enticing EA to move into the Chinese market to help the company attract consumers and ultimately increase its revenue (Yang 2007). Intel has also invested in the Chinese online game market. In early June 2004, the chip giant linked up with a major Shanghai-based online game operator, Shanda Networking Co. (Shanda), to jointly develop interactive entertainment infrastructure for playing online games with a variety of devices, including PCs, TV set-top boxes, and mobile phones (*China Daily* 2004). In addition, Shanda and TECMO, a Japanese developer, agreed to provide games, including the online version of the video game series *Dead or Alive*, to China. The two companies have merged and brought their individual strengths to the table in order to cocreate games. Shanda and TECMO recognized the endless possibilities between the two companies (Shanda 2007). Several European online game firms are also increasing their investment in China. For example, in 2007, Swedish gaming company MindArk PE AB signed a contract with Chinese game operator Cyber Recreation Development Corp. to introduce a virtual world game called *Entropia Universe* into China (China IT & Telecom Report 2007).

Taiwanese online corporations are also strategically pursuing transnationalization. In Taiwan, Gamania, the country's number one online gaming service company, which publishes games exclusively in Asia, has recently chosen Ultimus BPM Suite, a company based in the United States, to control its project management, purchasing, approval structure, and design approval processes (dBusinessNews 2007). Ultimus is the number-one provider of business process management as its technology adapts to people and is available in 16 different languages. This is an important event, because an Eastern gaming company is using a technology developed by a Western company, and the two markets are now working cooperatively. No longer are companies restricted to working and developing domestically; businesses around the world are blending, with projects and technologies being used interchangeably.

Most of all, the transnationalization of the domestic online game industry has occurred at a meteoric speed in Korea, because big national online game firms have drawn great interest from foreigners due to the massive increase in the number of online game players and game developers (Jin and Chee 2008). The effects of the transnationalization of the online game industry have been felt profoundly due to continuing foreign interests in large Korean game firms. Along with large domestic-based companies, foreign-based TNCs have invested in the Korean online game industry. As of August 2008, 14 major game publishers, including EA, Microsoft, THQ, SEGA, and Vivendi Universal, have their own branches in Korea (Korea Game Industry Agency 2008). In its most recent investment, EA invested $105 million in the Korean game company Neowiz, receiving 19% of the shares, for the codevelopment and global publishing of online games in 2007 (Cho, J. 2007b). EA also purchased a Korean online game developer, J2MSoft Inc., in December 2008, which shows EA's continuing interest in the Asian market. As Jon Niermann, president of EA Asia, states, "this is a significant step in EA's strategic plan for developing and publishing online games in Asia" (*Business Week* 2008). SEGA, a Japanese game maker, also has established an affiliation with SK Telecom, and, since 2008, it has expedited the localization of its online games, including *Splash Golf* (*Digital Times* 2008). Japanese console maker Nintendo also established a partnership with Nexon in 2006. Foreign investors were holding around half of the shares of major Korean game firms, such as NCsoft (41.8%) and NHN (51.4%) as of March 2007 (Cho, J. 2007b), but the share has decreased in 2008 and 2009 due to the global economic recession. In March 2007, Blizzard Entertainment, one of the biggest global game developers, also expressed its intention to work with Korean online game firms, and it has already opened a branch in Seoul to provide its own game programs to local users. Disney has also revealed its desire to build strategic partnerships with NCSoft and Nexon in the game area in 2009 (Choe 2009).

Prior to this, a Japanese technology company, Softbank, acquired a majority share of the Korean game developer Gravity for $409 million, the largest takeover thus far. Japan's SEGA entered a joint venture in

1996 with Hyundai Digital, a former subsidiary of the Hyundai Group, and they worked together on online games beginning in 2001. This is in addition to the penetration of the domestic market by subsidiaries of Sony, Nintendo, and Microsoft—the world's three largest console game makers.

TNCs have proliferated in Korea due to exponential profits and advanced technologies. As will be discussed in detail later, a few domestic online game companies, such as NCsoft and Webzen, have invested in foreign markets; however, they have been transnationalized by foreign investors as well. The Korea Game Industry Agency promotes foreign investments in the domestic game industry. When the Korea Game Industry Agency (2007b) held its third game trade and exhibition fair, known-as G-Star, in 2007, as many as 70 foreign game developers and publishers, including THQ and UbiSoft, visited Korea to check its investment opportunities, and 67 domestic game firms participated in the exhibition. Several of these foreign companies want to invest in the Korean market because they plan to secure the services of Korean online games in their countries. For example, CDC Games, which is one of the major Chinese online game firms, established its Korean branch in 2007 in order to import Korean online games, including *Prelude to War 3* and to conduct its service in the Chinese market.

As such, transnationalization has brought about foreign capital and technology, which are now part of domestic online game industries in several Asian countries. Due to the rapid growth in foreign capital, several Asian online game firms have developed their software and increased their market revenues. However, the meteoric speed of the transnationalization of Asian online game industries is not without a price. With the rapid investment from foreign-based TNCs in the online game industry, the Korean online game world demonstrates that original know-how and technology, as well as server technique, which are fundamental parts of the domestic online game industry, could be transferred to TNCs. In the case of China, the country's online game industry may never depend on the West for content, but Chinese firms increasingly depend on or are integrated into a system of transnational commerce, involving foreign capital, distribution channels, management expertise, and technology (Cao and Downing 2008). In this sense, China's game industry can never be free from global trade and finance

systems in which Western economies and TNCs constitute the fundamental structure (Kotz 2002).

As Dan Schiller (2007, 124) points out, independent capital in Asia
has spearheaded and cultivated video and computer games; however, not
surprisingly, megatransnational conglomerates commodify the emerging
new media sector. Though the number of independent production companies grows, they absorb high product risks and labor costs for the
giants, which maintain their control over the critical areas of finance and
distribution as in other cultural sectors (Mosco 1996, 109). As much as
online game software from Asia, particularly Korea and China, has
flourished in other countries, the TNCs have been a formidable force to
deal with due to their abilities to generate exponential profits and their
resources for advanced technology acquisition and development.

Local Online Games—Moving toward the Global

While foreign-based TNCs have rapidly expanded in the Asian online
game market, several local online game corporations, primarily in
Korea and China, gain insider status within regional and global markets
as they operate around the world. Now the local game industry has
adopted the localization process of non-Western culture in Western
societies. As discussed in chapter 7, adopting the major media firm idea
of "think globally, act locally" (Fung 2006), Asia-based online game
firms have initiated glocalization for their gaming businesses—opening
branches in Western countries, developing games with Western publishers in these Western areas, and purchasing Western online game
corporations.

To begin with, Be Technology, a Korean computer game company,
bought Kali, a U.S. developer of Internet gaming networks, in a $2
million stock deal in 1999. Kali was the world's largest provider of
network solutions for multiplayer games, and some of the most popular
games, such as *StarCraft*, *Quake*, and *Age of Empires*, were played on
its network. Be Technology operated an online gaming platform and
wanted to expand its reach to the world market (*Korea Herald* 1999).
It was the first time a Korean game company acquired a U.S. firm, but
it was only the beginning of the massive investment of Korean online
game companies in other countries. A handful of local online game

companies have learned the importance of the global market, and they capitalize on the globalization trend by adapting to the user's local taste. Several Korean game companies and other corporations have entered the Asian market and later the Western market.

Most of all, NCsoft—famous for its *Lineage* games—has become active in the transnationalization process as a Korean game developer. NCsoft has pursued a strategy of global infrastructure and local content because it believes that gaming is culture that should fit local taste (Bu 2007). As discussed in chapter 7, NCsoft has expanded its reach beyond Asia. NCsoft wanted to drastically expand its market beyond Korea and neighboring countries under its ambition to globalize. Against this backdrop, the firm opened branches and entered into joint ventures in Hong Kong, China, Japan, and, later, the United States and United Kingdom. MGame Corporation, starting from its first online game called *Dark Server* in the late 1990s, has also swiftly increased its presence in the global market; MGame currently has three branches—in Japan, the United States, and China—while partnering with nine foreign game corporations in Vietnam, China, Singapore, and Europe (MGame 2009). MGame's *YulGang*, one of the successful MMORPGs produced in Korea, earned 80% of its revenues from foreign countries as of July 2009 (*Digital Times* 2009). As the most recent investment in Asia, SK Telecom, Korea's top mobile carrier, has entered the fast-growing market in China in a bid to generate new income sources by expanding its business overseas. The company agreed to invest $7.8 million into the acquisition of a 30% stake in Magicgrids Networks, a China-based company specializing in developing and publishing online games (Jin and Chee 2008). In addition, several major online game developers and publishers, including Hanbit Soft, Webzen, NHN, and ACTOZSOFT, have established joint ventures with several Asian companies as part of their corporate strategies to penetrate Asian markets.

Meanwhile, Chinese online game corporations are penetrating Western markets. In 2003, Shanda acquired a nearly 20% interest in a Tokyo software developer, Bothtec Inc., which was the first instance of a Chinese firm buying into a Japanese game software house (*Nikkei Weekly* 2003). Several Chinese online game firms also directly financed through a NASDAQ listing in recent years. Instead of building branches or forming joint ventures with American online game firms, they have attracted foreign investors through the stock market because they acknowledge U.S. investors are interested in the Chinese online game industry.

The Asian online game corporations have penetrated other parts of the region and later the Western hemisphere. We often hear about Westernization and globalization in which Western culture is contemplating Eastern society, and where the West is heavily influencing the East in many aspects of life. While EA and many other Western companies are entering the Eastern markets, companies from Asia are also influencing the gaming world, which shows two-way transnationalization, as opposed to domination strictly from the West. The emergence of Asian game corporations in the global market has somewhat changed the contemporary concept of globalization by targeting and successfully penetrating not only regional but also Western countries. Asian online game firms recognize the opportunity they have with broadband and the online gaming experience; it is common for companies to sell their products to a worldwide audience.

However, it is premature to predict the impact of capital involvement from Korean online game companies (as non-Western TNCs) on the global market. Although several Asian corporations have initiated an invitation to foreign investors and developers as part of their globalization strategies, the result is not much different than the transnationalization process in other non-Western cultural industries. Except for a handful of big online game firms, the majority of Asian online game companies cannot join foreign markets due to their relatively small capital, which is a major hurdle in the globalization process of the local game industry. A few domestic online game companies in Asia have invested in the Western markets, but the majority of those in the online game industries are simply unable to break into foreign markets.

Transnationalization in the Realm of the People

In the realm of online gaming, users and jobseekers around the world are working and being recruited by companies outside their countries of origin. Because the language of the computer has neither boundary nor limitation, someone who originates from Asia can work for a Western company or vice versa. Job opportunities are increasing for those who work on the production of games. The transnationalization of online gaming also affects people and the opportunities it provides for communities around the globe in which no one is bound to their respective countries, and globalization allows people and companies to expand internationally.

The key point is who the major players (e.g., developers) are in the market. The flow of the people is much more complicated in the online game industry than in other areas because a few highly skilled workers could change the map of the industry, which means some global-level developers are targets of many online game corporations. EA respects the Asian markets; however, they are not buying out their competition but are instead hoping to work with companies and their skilled-game workers. Gaming developers and operators are now being recruited throughout the world to work on projects that may not be from their country of origin. Jobs are now global, and cultures are crossed. These movements of workers around the world are not restricted to the development of games but also can be seen at positions of leadership.

The major players are primarily Western-based developers and managers. EA and many other gaming companies, such as Blizzard, see the significant potential in Asia (and particularly in Korea and China), where they could increase their dominance through expansion. For example, as noted, EA acquired 19% of Korea's Neowiz in hopes of jointly developing online games with Korean game developers and operators in Asia. Korea has been the leader in the online game business, and, therefore, many skilled workers in the country are valuable commodities for transnational online game corporations.

As such, some TNCs have recruited Asian developers and skilled workers to penetrate the Asian and global markets; however, the reality is not the same in many cases, because when they enter the Asian market, they invest not only capital but also bring people. Due to advanced technologies and marketing skills in the West, local online game corporations are heavily dependent on their expertise with a few exceptions. For example, EA recently announced that their acclaimed franchise from EA DICE, *Battlefield*, is entering the online gaming market in Asia (Electronic Arts 2007). The key to this announcement is that the creators of EA DICE in Sweden will be partnered with the development teams at Neowiz Games in Seoul to create games in Asian markets. The game *Battlefield* has seen success in North American and European markets, and they are hoping to create the same magic in Asia, with the help of the team at Neowiz (Electronic Arts 2007).

In China, ZhengTu Network, headquartered in Shanghai, has publicly offered a $1 million bounty to any experienced game design director who is willing to relocate to Shanghai (McCormack 2007). Mikoishi, a premier game development studio in Singapore, also appointed two new members—Frank Brown as Chairman of the Board and Irene Chua as CEO of the company. Frank Brown and Irene Chua joined a foreign company to help them expand and improve. Irene Chua had been responsible for the setup and oversees operation of EA in Korea, Japan, Taiwan, Singapore, Malaysia, Thailand, Hong Kong, and China. Frank Brown led the MTV Network into Asia by buying out its existing television networks (Mikoishi 2007). Mikoishi has appointed them because they both have a great track record of broadening a company into a foreign market in order to increase their power.

Prior to this, several cultural sectors had advanced the transnationalization of people. For example, Sony, one of the largest console game producers, had Howard Stringer as the chairman and CEO of the company. In the world of online gaming, if a gaming operator, designer, or developer has a higher capability than a domestic worker does, they will be used regardless of where they reside. The ultimate goal for transnationalization in terms of the people involved is to help their respective companies expand more globally. Mikoishi is just one example of what many companies are hoping to do with their business plans, and, as Brown states, "they are producing a new generation of interactive entertainment for a global audience" (Mikoishi 2007). Likewise, many Asian online game companies have hired Western CEOs, developers, and marketers because they need advanced technologies and marketing strategies.

Even when Asian game companies opened their subsidiaries or joint ventures in the West, the situation was no different. They need to rely on Western developers who know their own culture for the success of their marketing in that area. In fact, when NCsoft opened NC Interactive in Austin, Texas, in 2000, it signed Richard Garriott, the U.S. game programmer best known for ULTIMA Online, and 19 others from Destination Games Inc., which was located in Austin (NCsoft 2007b). Several Asian game corporations have entered Western markets; however, they have had to recruit Western developers and marketing team members due to their advanced knowledge in developing, publishing, and marketing. Because the local culture embedded in online games is crucial for the success of special games in each region, local-based transnational game companies have relied more on Western workers overall.

The online game industry has been transnationalized on a large scale from companies merging, buying out, and working together and from people being recruited across the globe. Programmers are being used cooperatively across companies, but foreigners, in hopes of using their differences in knowledge to expand the product, are now occupying positions on the board. The end product and ultimate goal for transnationalization is the production of a game that will be played in the homes of gamers in the East and in the West. The flow of people, however, is unequal between the West and the East. In terms of people, the online game industry can never be free from Western influence, because Western TNCs constitute the fundamental structure of the industry (Kotz 2002).

Transnationalization of Financing: New Business Models

The methods of financing online game companies are diverse and unique. The online game industry has rapidly developed new revenue resources, from building new business models to financialization, referring to a pattern of capital accumulation in which profits accrue primarily through financial channels rather than through trade and commodity production (Krippner 2005). To begin with, several game corporations have developed new business and/or financing methods. Unlike the console game industry, many Asian online game companies attempt to pioneer a new economic model for online games, which lessens the operator's dependency on subscription costs. The major online game corporations, such as Blizzard, Webzen, and NCsoft, see the difference between the East and the West; therefore, they set up different types of payment methods for the two. In North America, gamers pay a set monthly fee so that during this period they can play as long as they want. However, in Asia, gaming cards are used, where hours are calculated and the gaming period is set for a certain amount of time depending on the card that is purchased. In China, the online payment system is in the early stages of adoption. Credit or debit card usage is still not popular among online game players. Hence, cash-based point card sales (both virtual and physical cards) have been the most popular payment method (Canadian Heritage 2008).[1] In addition, Webzen, a Korean gaming company, created a new business model for online games where their profit would come from gamers purchasing virtual items instead of subscription costs. The company hopes to deliver a game that earns premium profits by selling upgraded weaponry, experiences, and abilities to users who will pay more than the basic subscription to enhance their play (McCormack 2007).

These new concepts of profit are all derived from cultural differences observed around the world. The transnationalization of these gaming companies also means that they now have to take gamers across the globe into consideration and provide for everyone instead of a target niche. NCsoft has introduced a new global form of financial structuring for online games, which is another aspect of the globalization strategy. Until 2003, the online game norm in terms of the financial structure was that subscribers paid a monthly fee to play. For *Lineage [I]*, players pay a monthly fee and download the software. However, as discussed in chapter 7, *Lineage II* introduced sixty-day game time cards for a suggested retail price of $29.99, as well as a monthly subscription format. Several games followed what *Lineage II* introduced. For example, *Guild Wars*, developed by ArenaNet, used the same format, and *Guild Wars* cost approximately $50 for the basic version. The company also released an expansion pack every six months instead of charging for a subscription (Colbourne 2005).

Several Asian online game firms directly raise financing in the U.S. stock market. While the majority of online game firms accumulate capital through international trade and commodity production, several Asian online game firms have rapidly developed a new strategy of financialization. In the midst of competition between Chinese and Korean online game developers, several companies started to rush to the tech-heavy NASDAQ in the United States. Webzen, Korea's second largest online game developer, raised $97.2 million with a NASDAQ listing in December 2003 (*Korea Times* 2003). Gravity, another Korean online-game company, also wanted to expand internationally and became a NASDAQ member. In October 2004, Gravity hit a peak of more than 770,000 concurrent users in Japan, China, Korea, Canada, the United States, and various European countries. The company hoped to raise $88 million in the initial public offering for game development, while enhancing marketing, distribution, and service capabilities as a globally recognized online game developer (Kanellos 2005).

Successful public financing has stimulated other corporations as well, particularly Chinese online game firms. Shanda's rise and expansion heavily depended on its capacity to raise finances, mainly via NASDAQ (AsiaInfo Services 2004). Shanda's stock had risen from $11 in 2004 to more than $30 as of January 18, 2005 (Kanellos 2005). Successful global financing enabled Shanda to engage in a series of acquisitions, including its acquisition of 29% of the stocks of ACTOZ, one of Korea's largest online game companies (Cao and Downing 2008). Another mammoth online game operator in China, The9 Ltd., also raises financing through a NASDAQ listing. These companies have the same immediate goal—to enhance the recognition of investors in the firm and to make money, regardless of their different long-term goals.

Financialization of the Asian online game industry entails a range of elements, including neoliberal economic doctrines such as deregulation and liberalization. The growth of financialization has been routinely presented as a reality-driven liberalization of markets; that is, in the midst of neoliberal reform, Asian countries have had to open their markets, and some of them are actively involved in the transnationalization and globalization process (Greenfield and Williams 2007). Due to the norm of global liberalization, several Asian online game firms directly finance through the U.S. stock market. Although this new financing system has brought a vast amount of money to these online game firms, it also proves that, more or less, Asian online game industries are increasingly dependent on or integrated into a system of transnational commerce, including foreign capital, as well as distribution channels, management expertise, and technology (Cao and Downing 2008).

In sum, the online gaming market has created a blend of companies that is capable of crossing cultures and language barriers to provide gaming experiences for gamers around the world. Companies are being bought out, invested in, or are working cooperatively across the globe, where there is no longer a barrier that restricts companies to work only in their own domestic market. Companies are going global with shops set up in countries around the world using programmers and technologies while developing new financing models in specific areas in order to develop the most consumer-attractive game possible. However, the transnationalization and globalization process is not equal. With a few exceptions, Western-based online game firms have more power than Asian corporations due to their advanced capital system and marketing strategies, as well as their workforce.

Summary

This chapter discusses a shifting trend in the transnationalization process of the online game industry, focusing on why and how transnationalization has become a unique phenomenon in the midst of globalization. Online game development has gone from being a cottage industry in the 1980s to a global industry. Only a decade ago, the online game industry was known as the ultimate cottage industry, with companies employing fewer than 20 employees on average and having limited funds available for the development of new games, but it has become one of the major parts of the global cultural industry. As Murdock and Golding (1997) point out, all media industries have gone through a process of growth, from small-scale production to large concentrated corporations, and the online game industry is one such example. This process happens because capitalism tends to encourage concentration, whereby a small number of firms effectively control enough of the market to manipulate it in their favor (Garnham 1990). As in the film industry, the most significant feature of TNCs is the general business activity abroad, which includes direct production, distribution, and local labor. In order to achieve this goal, TNCs usually establish affiliates abroad and acquire the ownership and control of their assets (Letto-Gillies 2005).

The online game industry has shown unique characteristics that differ markedly from other cultural industries in terms of transnationalization and globalization in the twenty-first century. The game industry has proven that online game firms, not only from the United States but also from non-Western countries, particularly Asian countries, have played key roles. Asian-based online game companies, alongside Western corporations as key players in the global market, have initiated and influenced the global transnationalization scene. How the online game industry differs from the film industry is that there are fewer dominant major Western companies than in the film sector of the global market. There are several American online game companies playing key roles in the transnationalization process of the global online game industry, including EA and Blizzard Entertainment; however, Asian online game companies have also swiftly become involved in the globalization process, as a reflection of their leading roles in the online game industry. Several game companies in Korea, China, and Taiwan have initiated the transnationalization process, meaning they have invested in the European market as well as in the American market, while they actively invite foreign capital into their domestic game operations. The online game industry has experienced a relatively strong presence of the Asian game industry in Western countries, which might suggest that the online game center in the world now consists of possibly two megaplayers: the United States and Asia. The transnationalization of the online game industry has certainly challenged traditional boundaries between the West and the East, and has questioned the principle of Western dominance in the cultural market.

It is suggested that transnationalization has brought the merging of companies, people, and games from all over the world. No longer are people and companies restricted to their domestic countries, but interactions and transactions are possible around the world. As the online game industry no longer addresses national game players, it has exponentially transnationalized in terms of capital investment, trade, people, and new financing. Several theoreticians argue that mass media hegemony, once a matter of one national culture dominating another, can no longer explain the national character of the institutions of mass media. Through transnationalization, this new trend seems to apply in the online game industry. It might very well be true that the current strategies of these Western online game companies no longer allow for a special dominance in the global market. While mega companies based in the United States and a few Western countries have dominated the film and broadcasting industries ever since the beginning of the postwar era in several ways, including coproductions and foreign direct investment, the online game industry has been a battleground between Western and non-Western countries. Transnationalization among the players of the online gaming industry has seen transactions between companies originate all around the world. The dynamic cultural traffic in the online game industry may provide a scenario that it is freeing itself from Western power, but it is too early to confirm this.

The issue, then, is the degree of penetration of the Asian game industry, and, therefore, the remaining unequal flow of production, people, and capital. Although several Asian online game firms have penetrated other countries with their advanced games, when it comes to some major areas, such as capital, skilled workers, and management systems, Western developers and publishers are the major players. In the online game industry, theories of dependency and cultural imperialism, in spite of being under heavy attack, still have some explanatory power through their pinpointing of the clear dependency of the Asian online game industry, especially regarding capital, distribution, and technology transfer (Cao and Downing 2008). All evidence indicates that the transnationalization of the online game industry will continue to not only deepen the ongoing process of the commodification of this new Asian culture and media sector, but also to subordinate to transnational corporations seeking profits. Because Western-based online game firms have more capital, skills, and people armed with advanced marketing expertise, their influence remains powerful, although it is less dominant than in other cultural sectors. Therefore, how to establish a balance between domestic and foreign forces in the production and distribution of Korean online games is one of the major challenges in maintaining or continuing the country's status as the online game empire in the global game market.

Notes

Chapter 1

1. As discussed in detail in chapter 7, this book positions Japan as a Western country, based on its economy, technology, and culture. Therefore, Japanese console games are considered Western cultural products. Location is no longer a major factor in deciding whether a country is Western or Eastern.

Chapter 2

1. For example, Lee and others (2003) mention that the strong emphasis on education and academic performance has prompted parents to turn to the Internet for educational goods and services; however, they do not extend their discussion further.

2. The Korean government, starting in February 2008, abolished the Ministry of Information and Communication in the midst of the structural reorganization of the government system. The major function of the Ministry of Information and Communication has been carried over to several different organizations, including the Korea Communications Commission, which is responsible for broadcasting and telecommunications policies.

3. The government placed an emphasis on creating Internet-friendly classrooms at every level of schooling by connecting them to high-speed Internet free of charge as the main component of educational information infrastructure. The government spent $1.4 billion for the establishment of school information infrastructure between 1998 and late 2000. Of this amount, the government used $600 million to connect classrooms of 10,064 elementary, middle, and high schools around the country with broadband services (Lim 2001, 3).

4. KT, a government-owned telecommunication corporation in Korea, was privatized in May 2002. KT was a monopoly fixed-line local telephone service, which accounted for 96.9% of the market in March 2002. At the end of March 2002, KT also had an 86% share in the long-distance calling market and a 64% share in the international calling market. KT has rapidly invested in broadband services and has become the largest player in Korea (Jin 2006; *Korea Times* 2002).

5. Hanaro Telecom was purchased by SK Telecom and turned into SK Broadband in September 2008. Although SK Broadband began its business in the broadband market, its market share has not changed much. As of April 2009, KT maintains the largest market share (42.7%), followed by SK Broadband (23.2%), LG Powercom (14.6%), and cable service operators and others (Korea Communications Commission 2009).

6. 100 Mbps broadband services can download the equivalent of a 32-page newspaper per second and a film (1.4 GB) within 2 minutes, compared to 1 hour with 3.5 Mbps broadband services.

7. Parks Associates surveyed over ten thousand households in thirteen countries and ranked nations according to their proclivity to adopt and use MP3 players, video-on-demand, home networks, computers, online services, and similar advanced technologies. The survey found that Taiwan (Digital Living Index: 8.7) and Korea (8.4) lead the world in the adoption of consumer technologies, followed by the United States (8.1), Canada (8.0), and Japan (7.9) (Parks Associates 2005).

Chapter 3

1. The Korean government has conducted another systematic change to consolidate relevant content agencies, including the Korean Game Industry Agency, into one agency. The government established the Korean Creative Content Agency to effectively support content industries in May 2009. In order to provide information about the historical change of the development to the readers, this book maintains the old names instead of using the new names.

Chapter 4

1. Michael Wagner claims that the emergence of eSports is usually associated with the release of networked FPS games; in particular, the 1993 released game *Doom* and the 1996 follow-up title *Quake* by id software in the United States and Europe. However, eSports actually began its history in Australia and later Korea (see Wagner 2006).

Chapter 5

1. Another theoretical framework that should be mentioned is the relationship between games and serious life. By analyzing Johan Huizinga's (1938) study Homo Ludens, Hector Rodriguez (2006) addresses the relationship between games as play and as serious life from a cultural studies perspective, which is useful. Although Rodriguez' essay makes a great contribution to developing the critical juncture of play and seriousness, this chapter primarily analyzes the demographical characteristics of pro gamers as a labor force and the commodification process of them from a political economy perspective.

2. As discussed in chapter 4, eSports was originally used as a narrow definition of electronic sports leagues that competed through network games; however, with the growth of online games, eSports includes not only competition through network games but also cultural and industrial activities related to network games (Korea Game Industry Agency 2006).

3. *Special Force* is an online FPS developed by Dragon Play in 2004, and Special Force Pro League is the first professional league with online games produced in Korea, unlike other professional leagues, who use online games developed in other countries, such as *StarCraft*. Unlike previous professional leagues, only eight teams are participating in the Special Force Pro League in its early stages, including three semi-professional teams (RePute, nL. BeST, and Archer).

4. The first several professional teams did not have major sponsors. Coaches used their own money to manage the teams. When pro gamers won competitions and received awards, they shared part of the money with the team. Players participated in some events offered by large *PC bangs* and universities to help fund the teams. Pro gamers on these teams did not make much money, and large corporations have easily taken over these small teams.

Chapter 6

1. As a reflection of the rapid growth of Web 2.0 technologies, including social networks (e.g., MySpace, Weblogs, Twitter, and Facebook), several articles have paid attention to users as labor forces in relation to participatory culture (Nakamura 2009; Suhr 2009; Pedersen 2008; Cote and Pybus 2007; Theberge 2005). Only a few of them emphasize fan club members and/or online game players as labor forces who serve advertisers and corporations, either voluntarily or involuntarily. These previous works have not reviewed the major role of fans and gamers as commodities, regardless of the fact that online game fans are comparable to television audiences and readers of newspapers.

2. In fact, with the rapid technological changes and digitalization impacting the culture industries, several scholars have proposed different expressions replacing the term "audience." Most of all, Sonia Livingstone, among others, advocates replacing the term "audience" altogether with the more explicitly (inter)active term "user." She emphasizes the action of being an audience/user, literally emphasizing the verbs involved: "These media and information technologies open up new, more active modes of engagement with media—playing computer games, surfing the Web, searching databases, writing and responding to email, visiting a chat room, shopping online, and so on" (Livingstone 2003, 355).

3. This figure comes from the Daum Café (www.cafe.daum.net) and its fan clubs on January 23, 2009. Although there are several other Web portals hosting fan clubs, this chapter only uses Daum because it is the most reliable resource for the figure. Some movie and sports stars have several different fan clubs, of course; however, it only selects the largest and most popular fan club at the café.

4. Terranova developed a thesis that she called free labor—namely, that free labor is a central feature of both the Internet and informationalized economy. Free labor is a feature of the cultural economy at large and an important, yet unacknowledged, source of value in advanced capitalist societies. Free labor on the Internet includes the activity of building Web sites, modifying software packages, reading and participating in mailing lists, and building virtual spaces (Terranova 2004, 73–74).

5. As explained in chapter 5, in April 2009, the Korea e-Sport Association started a new game league called Special Force Pro League, and SK Telecom as a sponsor financially supports the league. Unlike other game leagues, the Special Force Pro League supports clans, which are gamer mania communities, by providing some money for their activities. For example, several clans that are game communities organized by game users, instead of pure fans, actively participate in the league because they, as game users, are also competing with each other. In particular, Neowiz, the game service provider of the *Special Force* game, organizes a so-called The Best Clan event to attract more clan members. Neowiz gives medals to the top 100 clans, while providing monetary rewards for the best two clans ($500). Through this event, clan members become lucrative commodities for Neowiz and SK Telecom, which intend to utilize clan members as well as game fans (Lee, S.H. 2009).

6. The idea of the audience commodity is straightforward: "readers and audience members of advertising-supported mass media are a commodity produced and sold to advertisers because they perform a valuable service for the advertisers" (Smythe 1981, 8). In short, the audience is not a category like class, gender, or race; rather, it is an aggregation of people linked to a particular market, be it for a cultural commodity (such as a television program) or the commodities advertised therein (Cote and Pybus 2007, 97).

Chapter 7

1. Periphery theory has heavily relied on core-periphery theory, which is based on the notion that as one state or a few advanced states expands in economic prosperity, it must engulf regions nearby to ensure ongoing economic and political success. However, Immauel Wallerstein (1974) contested that the core-periphery system is far too simple, and the semiperiphery is also a significant middle ground between the core and the periphery. He divided the world economy into three areas, including core, semiperiphery, and periphery societies. Core societies are powerful industrial countries that exercise economic domination, and, by the end of the twentieth century, the core was comprised exclusively of wealthy industrialized countries, including the United States, the United Kingdom, France, Germany, and Japan. Some countries labeled semiperipheral are Mexico, Brazil, Korea, India, and China.

2. Some of the largest and most viable online communities to date are the persistent, open-ended, graphically intensive, and three-dimensional online environments known variously as massively multiplayer online games, MMORPGs, and virtual worlds (see Malaby 2006, 144).

3. Due to the rapid growth of several console makers, including Sega, Sony, and Nintendo, Consalvo (2006) claims that cultural imperialism no longer explains the Japanese cultural market, because Japanese popular culture shows its unique contra-cultural flow, from a non-Western country to the West. However, several scholars, such as Stuart Hall (1996), Herbert Schiller (1976), and Immanuel Wallerstein (1974), have made cases that Japan should be considered a major part of the West, based on its advanced economy, technology, and modernization. Therefore, whether console gaming is a case of contra-flow is not fully endorsed in media studies.

Chapter 8

1. Physical cards are scratch cards with passcodes printed on them. After scratching the card, players enter the pin to recharge the game account. Operators incur manufacturing and inventory costs for physical cards. A virtual card is essentially a list of passcodes. Players usually pay cash to a Web café, after which the cashier writes the passcode on a piece of paper (or, in some cases, the cashier will charge the gamers' account directly). Large operators have their own proprietary eSales system, which tracks virtual card transactions from operators to different levels of distributors and then finally sales at Web cafés.

References

Aizu, Izumi. 2002. A comparative study on broadband in Asia: Development and policy. Paper presented at the Asian Economic Integration—Current Status and Prospects, Symposium hosted by RIETI on April 22.

An, Jun Hyun. 2001. English education special: Let's play with English online. *HanKook Ilbo*, August 27, 2001, 26.

Anderson, Craig, Jeanne B. Funk, and Mark Griffiths. 2004. Contemporary issues in adolescent video game playing: Brief overview and introduction to the special issue. *Journal of Adolescence* 27(1):1–3.

Andrejevic, Mark. 2004. *Reality TV: The work of being watched*. Lanham, Md.: Rowman & Littlefield.

———. 2007. *Ispy: Surveillance and power in the interactive era*. Lawrence, Kans.: University Press of Kansas.

———. 2008. Watching television without pity: The productivity of online fans. *Television and New Media* 9(1):24–46.

Artz, Lee. 2008. Media relations and media products: Audience commodity. *Democratic Communiqué* 22(1):60–74.

AsiaInfo Services. 2004. Shanda to list in Nasdaq in May. Available at http://www.highbeam.com/doc/1P1-93960351.html

Back, Kang Reung. 2005. SK Telecom triggers first. *Chosun Ilbo*, May 31, 2005.

Bajaj, Vikas. 2002. High-speed connections common in South Korea. *Seattle Times*, October 21, 2002.

Baldwin, Thomas, F. McVoy, D. Stevens, and Charles W. Steinfield. 1996. *Convergence: Integrating media, information, and communication*. Thousand Oaks, Calif.: Sage.

Barlett, Christopher, and Sumantra Ghoshal. *Managing Across Borders*. London: Random House Business Books, 1998.

Barriault, Andre. 2005. NCsoft names new producers for *Lineage II*. Available at http://www.hoovers.com/free/co/factsheet.xhtml?COID=117239&cm_ven=PAID&cm_cat=YAH&cm_pla=CO4&cm_ite=ncsoft

Belson, Ken, and Matt Richtel. 2003. America's broadband dream is alive in Korea. *New York Times,* May 5, 2003, C1.

Betanews. 2009. KT inroads Vietnam with online games, March 7, 2009. Available at http:www.betanews.net

Borgmann, Albert. 1984. *Technology and the character of contemporary life.* Chicago, Ill.: University of Chicago Press.

Boyd-Barrett, Oliver. 2006. Cyberspace, globalization and empire. *Global Media and Communication* 2(1):21–41.

Bu, Hung Kwon. 2007. *Lineage,* 680 times increase in sales over the last ten years. *Dong-a Ilbo,* April 4, 2007, 44.

Buckingham, David. 2006. Studying computer games. In *Computer games: Text, narrative and play,* ed. C. Diane, D. Buckingham, A. Burn, and G. Schott, 1–13. Malden, Mass.: Polity.

Business Week. 2008. Electronic Arts buys Korean online game developer, December 3, 2008.

Caddell, Bud. 2008. The fan economy: Becoming fan focused. Available at http://budcaddell.com

Canada Broadcasting Corporation. 2007. *Gamer revolution I. February 1 & 7.* Ottawa: CBC.

Canadian Heritage. 2008. The Chinese video game market: Market entry for Canadian firms. Available at http://www.pch.gc.ca/progs/ac-ca/progs/rc-tr/pubs/chin_vid/4_e.cfm

Cao, Yang, and John D.H. Downing. 2008. The realities of virtual play: Video games and their industry in China. *Media Culture & Society* 30(4):515–529.

Carr, Diane, David Buckingham, Andrew Burn, and Schott Gareth. 2006. *Computer games: Text, narrative and play.* Malden, Mass.: Polity.

Castells, Manuel. 1996. *The rise of the network society.* Cambridge, Mass.: Blackwell Publishers.

———. 2001. *The Internet galaxy: Reflection on the Internet, business and society.* Oxford: Oxford University Press.

Chalaby, Jean K. 2007. Beyond nation-centrism: Thinking international communication from cosmopolitan perspective. *Studies in Communication Sciences* 7(1):61–83.

Chambers, Todd, and Herbert Howard. 2005. The economics of media consolidation. In *Handbook of media management and economics,* ed. Alan B. Albarran, Sylvia M. Chan-Olmsted, and M. Wirth, 363–386. Mahwah, N.J.: Lawrence Erbaum.

Chan, Dean. 2008. Negotiating online computer games in East Asia: Manufacturing Asian MMORPGs and marketing Asianess. In *Computer games as a sociocultural phenomenon: Games without frontiers war without tears,* ed. Andreas Jahn-Sudmann and Ralf Stocmann, 186–196. New York: Palgrave.

Chang, Jae Soon. 1999. Professional computer game players believe they are not just killing time. *Korea Herald,* July 31, 1999.

Chan-Olmsted, Sylvia M. 1998. Mergers, acquisitions, and convergence: The strategic alliance of broadcasting, cable television, and telephone services. *Journal of Media Economics* 11(3):33–46.

Chee, Florence. 2006. The games we play online and offline: Making Wang-tta in Korea. *Popular Communication* 4(3):225–239.

China Daily. 2004. Intel, Shanda to jointly develop digital home technology, June 9, 2004.

China IT & Telecom Report. 2007. Swedish game company enters China market with virtual world, June 8, 2007.

Chinese Cultural Connection. 1987. Chinese values and the search for culture-free dimensions of culture. *Journal of Cross-Cultural Psychology* 18(2):143–164.

Cho, Hyo Young. 2002. 5-day workweek to spotlight new software sectors: SERI. *Korea Herald*, November 9, 2002.

Cho, Jin Se. 2005a. Games making 2nd Korean wave. *Korea Times*, December 12, 2005.

Cho, Jin Se. 2007a. Hangame meets Japanese taste. *Korea Times*, December 17, 2007.

———. 2007b. US game giant EA to invest $100 M in Korean game. *Korea Times*. March 20, 2007.

Cho, Soo Hee. 2009. *StarCraft, Lineage, KartRider*, and thereafter. *KIS Credit Monitor*, February 9, 2009.

Cho, S. Y. 2005. Positive and negative aspects of the pro-game world. *Game DongA*. May 5, 2005.

Choe, Bung Jun. 2009. Korean game dominates Asian markets, towards the globe. May 21, 2009. Available at http://www.zdnet.co.kr

Choi, Ho Kyung. 2010. Korea Creative Content Agency announces its Investment in 2010. *Game DongA*. 24 February.

Chosun Ilbo. 2008. High-speed Internet becomes more faster. August 13, 2008.

Chosun Ilbo. 2009. CJ-Onmedia will challenge network broadcasters. June 22, 2009.

Choudrie, Jyoti, and Hee Jin Lee. 2004. Broadband development in South Korea: Institutional and cultural factors. *European Journal of Information Systems* 13(2):103–114.

Christians, Cliff G. 1989. A theory of normative technology. In *Technological transformation: Contextual and conceptual implications*, ed. Edmund F. Byrne and Joseph C. Pitt, 123–139. Dordrecht: Kluwer Academic Publishers.

Chung, Peichi. 2008. New media for social change: Globalization and the online gaming industries of South Korea and Singapore. *Science, Technology & Society* 13(2):303–323.

CJ Internet. 2009. Company overview. Available at http://www.cjinternet.com

Colbourne, Scott. 2005. The on-line lineup: Guild wars. *Globe and Mail*, May 6, 2005, R33.

Coleman, Sarah, and N. Dyer-Witheford. 2007. Playing on the digital commons: Collectivities, capital and contestation in videogame culture. *Media Culture & Society* 29(6):934–953.

ComScore. 2007. Worldwide online gaming community reaches 217 million people, July 10, 2007. Press Release. Available at http://www.comscore.com/press/release.asp?press=1521

Consalvo, Mia. 2006. Console video games and global corporations: Creating a hybrid culture. *New Media & Society* 8(10):117–137.

———. 2007. *Cheating: Gaining advantage in videogames*. Cambridge, Mass.: MIT Press.

Cote, Mark, and Jennifer Pybus. 2007. Learning to Immaterial Labour 2.0: MySpace and social networks. *ephemera: theory and politics in organization* 7(1):88–106.

Crawford, Garry, and Jason Rutter. 2006. Digital games and cultural studies. In *Understanding digital games*, ed. Jason Rutter and Jo Bryce, 148–165. London: Sage.

Crotty, James, and Kang Kook Lee. 2002. A political-economic analysis of the failure of neo-liberal restructuring in post-crisis Korea. *Cambridge Journal of Economics* 26(5):667–678.

dBusinessNews. 2007. Taiwan leading online gaming services company selects Ultimus. Available at http://triangle.dbusinessnews.com/shownews.php?newsid=124188&type_news=latest

Deuze, Mark, Chase Bowen Martin, and Christina Allen. 2007. The professional identity of gameworkers. *International Journal of Research into New Media Technologies* 13(4):335–353.

Digital Times. 2008. SK Telecom works with SEGA, June 23, 2008.

———. 2009. Special Force Pro-league starts, April 2, 2009.

Drucker, Peter F. 1967. *Technology, management and society*. New York: Harper and Row.

Dyer-Witheford, Nick. 2004. Mapping the Canadian video and computer game industry. Kingston, Ontario, A Talk for the Digital Poetics and Politics Summer Institute, Queen's University.

Dyer-Witheford, Nick, and Greig de Peuter. 2006. EA spouse and the crisis of video game labor: Enjoyment, exclusion, exploitation, exodus. *Canadian Journal of Communication* 31:599–617.

Dyer-Witheford, Nick, and Zena Sharman. 2005. The political economy of Canada's video and computer game industry. *Canadian Journal of Communication* 30:187–210.

Economic Review. 2004. Online game dominates the world. Available at http://www.ermedia.net/news/viewbody.php?uid=2872&ho=211&category=0

Economist. 1997. Babes with guns: Britain's videogame industry. February 22, 1997, 74–75.

Electronic Arts. 2007. Acclaimed franchise from EA DICE co-developed with Neowiz Games to expand EA's online offering in Asia, June 6, 2007. Press Release.

Electronic Daily. 2009. Change the games from poison to beneficial medicine. April 23, 2009.

Ellul, Jacques. 1964. *The technological society*. New York: Vintage.

Entertainment Software Association. 2007. *Industry facts*. Available at http://www.theesa.com/facts/index.asp

Entertainment Software Association of Canada. 2009. *Canada's entertainment software industry*. Ottawa, Ontario: Hickling Arthurs Low.

Featherstone, Mike, ed. 1990. *Global culture: Nationalism, globalization and modernity*. London: Sage.

Feenberg, Andrew. 1991. *Critical theory of technology*. New York: Oxford University.

Feller, Gordon, and Mary McNamara. 2003. Korea's broadband multimedia marketplace, March 26, 2003. Available at http://www.birds-eye.net/international/korea_gaming_market.shtml

Fiske, John. 1989. *Understanding popular culture*. London: Routledge.

Fitzgerald, Robert. 2005. Massively social technology. Available at http://www/ssat-inet.net/resources/olc/papers/massivelysocialtechnology.aspx

Florida, Richard. 2002. *The rise of the creative class*. New York: Basic.

Franklin, Ursula. 1999. *The real world of technology*. Toronto: Anansi.

French, Howard W. 2002. Korea's real rage for virtual games. *New York Times*, October 9, 2002.

Fung, Anthony. 2006. Think globally, act locally: China's rendezvous with MTV. *Global Media and Communication* 2(1):71–88.

Funk, Jeanne B. 2002. Video games grow up: Electronic games in the 21st century. In *Children, adolescents, and the media*. ed. Victor C. Strasburger and Barbara Wilson, 118–141. London: Sage.

Game Chosun. 2008. Cell phone purchasing pattern, October 14, 2008.

Game Developer. 2009. Game developer salary survey. Press Release. April 30, 2009.

Games Press. 2008. World Cyber Games 2008. Available at http://www.gamesindustry.biz/articles/world-cyber-games-2008-to-be-fought-out-on-samsung-monitors

Gamma, Seven. 2001. The world's largest game tournament kicks off at the 1st World Cyber Games. Available at http://news.bbc.co.uk/1/hi/world/asia-pacific/2499957.stm

Garnham, Nicholas. 1990. *Capitalism and communication: Global culture and the economics of information*. London: Sage.

————. 2000. *Emancipation, the media and modernity*. New York: Oxford University Press.

Giddens, Anthony. 1999. Runaway world: 1999 Reith lecture. Available at http://news.bbc.co.uk/hi/english/static/events/reith_99/week1/week1.htm

Gill, Rosalind. 2002. Cool, creative and egalitarian? Exploring gender in project-based new media work in Europe. *Information Communication and Society* 5(1):70–89.

Goodale, Gloria. 2008. Video-gaming strives for respect. Is it a sport? *Christian Science Monitor.* August 5, 2008.

Greenfield, Cathy, and Peter Williams. 2007. Financialization, finance rationality and the role of media in Australia. *Media Culture & Society* 29(3):415–433.

Grimes, Sara. 2006. Online multiplayer games: A virtual space for intellectual property debates. *New Media & Society* 8(6):969–990.

Grimes, Sara, and Andrew Feenberg. 2009. Rationalization play: A critical theory of digital gaming. *Information Society* 25(2):105–118.

Guback, Thomas. 1969. *The U.S. international film industry*. Bloomington: Indiana University Press.

Guback, Thomas. 1984. International circulation of U.S. theatrical films and television programming. In *World communications: A handbook*, ed. George Gerbner and Marsha Siefert, 153–163. New York: Longman.

Gunkel, David, and Hetzel Gunkel. 2009. Terra Nova 2.0—The new world of MMORPGs. *Critical Studies in Media Communication* 26(2):104–127.

Ha, A. Young. 2007a. Pro-gamer annual salary less than $10.000. *Hangyrae Shinmun*, April 24, 2007.

————. 2007b. Being the second Lim Yo-Hwan: Practice 14 hours without meals. *Hangyrae Shinmun*, April 24, 2007.

Hall, Stuart. 1996. The West and the rest. In *Modernity: An introduction to modern societies*, ed. Stuart Hall, David Held, and Kenneth Thompson, 185–227. Malden: Blackwell.

Ham, Sun Jin. 2003. Domestic game market to be $10 Billion: The government announced the long term plan. *Hangaeyae Shinmun*, November 13, 2003, 31.

Hamelink, Cees. 1983. *Cultural autonomy in global communications*. New York: Longman.

Han, Cho, and Hae Jung. 2006. Internet and culture: About the formation of subject in information society. Available at http://about.haja.net/bbs/download .asp?ClubNumber=2147483569&BoardType=3&file=119%08&code _generation=Ecce_Homo

Han, Gwang Jub. 2003. Broadband adoption in the United States and Korea: Business driven rational model versus culture sensitive policy model. *Trends in Communications* 11(1):3–25.

Heidegger, Martin. 1977. *The question concerning technology*, trans. W. Lovitt. New York: Harper and Row.

Hjorth, Larissa, and Dean Chan. 2009. *Gaming cultures and place in Asia-Pacific*. London: Routledge.

Hua, Vanessa. 2006. Video game players score big money in South Korea, SFGate.com. Available at http://sfgate.com/cgi-bin/article.cgi

Huhh, Jun Suk. 2009. The bang where Korean online gaming began: The culture and business of the PC bang in Korea. In *Gaming cultures and place in Asia-Pacific*, ed. Larissa Hjorth and Dean Chan, 102–116. London: Routledge.

Huizinga, Johan. *Home Ludens*. Mansfield, MI: Beacon Press, 1938.

Hutchins, Brett. 2008. Signs of meta-change in second modernity: The growth of e-sport and the World Cyber Games. *New Media & Society* 10(6):851–869.

Hwang, Si Young. 2007. More parents, women play computer games. *Korea Herald*, March 6, 2007.

Ieon. 2007. Bring back *A*mazing* to Australian television. Available at http://www.gopetition.com.au/petitions/bring-back-a-mazing-to-australian-television.html

IMDB. 1994. Plot summary of *A*mazing*. Available at http://www.imdb.com/title/tt0823638/plotsummary

International Telecommunication Union. 2003a. *Broadband Korea: Internet case study*. Paris: International Telecommunication Union.

International Telecommunication Union. 2003b. Number of global broadband subscribers grows 72% in 2002. Press Release. Paris: International Telecommunication Union, September 16, 2003.

Internet World Stats. 2008. World Internet users and population stats. Available at http://www.internetworldstats.com/stats.htm

Ip, Barry. 2008. Technological, content, and market convergence in the game industry. *Games and Culture* 3(2):199–224.

Ishii, Kenichi. 2003. Diffusion, policy, and use of broadband in Japan. *Trends in Communication* 11(1):45–61.

Iwabuchi, Koichi. 2002. *Recentering globalization: Popular culture and Japanese transnationalism*. Durham, N.C.: Duke University Press.

Jang, Jung Hun. 2007. Pro gamers' annual salary over $250,000. *Joong Ang Ilbo Blog*, September 19, 2007. Available at http:blog.joins.com/media/index.asp

Jenkins, Henry. 1992. *Textual poachers: Television fans and participatory culture*. London: Routledge.

———. 2002. Interactive audience? In *The new media book*, ed. Dan Harries, 157–170. London: BFI Publishing.

———. 2003. Quentin Tarantino's Star Wars: Digital cinema, media convergence, and participatory culture. In *Rethinking media change: the aesthetics of transition*, ed. David Thorburn and Henry Jenkins, 281–312. Cambridge, Mass.: MIT Press.

————. 2006. *An occasional paper on digital media and learning: Confronting the challenges of participatory culture: Media education for the 21st century.* Chicago, Ill.: The Macarthur Foundation.

Jeon, Gyong Ran. 2004. A study on the actualization of interactive text: Analysis of the massively multiplayer online role playing game playing. *Journal of Korean Communication* 48(5):188–213.

Jeong, Hyeon Ji. 2008. Copyright industry expands into global market. *Korea Herald,* August 2, 2008.

Jeong, Kuk Hwan, and King J. Leslie. 1997. Korea's national information infrastructure: Vision and issues. In *National information infrastructure initiatives: Vision and policy designs,* ed. Brian Kahin and Ernest J. Wilson III, 112–116. Cambridge, Mass.: MIT Press.

Jhally, Sut. 1987. *The codes of advertising: Fetishism and the political economy of meaning in the consumer society.* London: F. Pinter.

Ji, Bong Chul. 2003. Blockbuster games come. *Kyunghyung Games* 84(July): 29.

Jin, Dal Yong. 2005. Socio-economic implications of broadband services: Information economy in Korea. *Information Communication and Society* 8(4): 503–523.

————. 2006. Political and economic processes in the privatization of the Korean telecommunications industry: A case study of Korea Telecom, 1987-2003. *Telecommunications Policy* 30(1):3–13.

————. 2009. De-convergence: A shifting business trend in the U.S. digital media industries. *Journal of Media Economics and Culture* 7(1):3–44.

————. 2010. *Hands on/hands off: The Korean state and the market liberalization of the communication industry.* Cresskill, N.J.: Hampton Press.

Jin, Dal Yong, and Florence Chee. 2008. Age of new media empire: A critical interpretation of the Korean online game industry. *Games and Culture: A Journal of Interactive Media* 3(1):38–58.

Jin, Dal Yong, and Florence Chee. 2009. The politics of online gaming. In *Gaming cultures and place in Asia-Pacific,* ed. Larisa Hjorth and Dean Chan, 19–38. London: Routledge.

Jin, Hyun Joo. 2008. Naver launches IPTV. *Korea Herald.* January 29, 2008.

Jin, Hyung Joo. 2008. SK Telecom makes foray into Chinese gaming market. *Korea Herald,* May 16, 2008.

JoongAng Ilbo. 2009. Domestic online games become global games, June 17, 2009.

Joongang Ilbo English Edition. 2002. Generation 2030 went from apathy to passion, December 21, 2002.

Ju, Hae Lim. 2007. Online game market: Women drive new wind. *WomenNews,* June 8, 2007.

Jung, Dae Hoon. 2006. EG established estro, pro game team, October 14, 2006. Available at http://www.ohmynews.com/NWS_Web/View/at_pg.aspx ?CNTN_CD=A0000366391

Jung, Sung Ki. 2006. Air Force to recruit online gamers. *Korea Times*, March 22, 2006.

Kanellos, Michael. 2005. Korea online gaming firm files for U.S. IPO, January 20, 2005. *CNET News*. Available at http://news.cnet.com/Korean-online-gaming -firm-files-for-U.S.-IPO/2100-1043_3-5544093.html

Kerr, Aphra. 2006a. *The business and culture of digital games: Gamework/ gameplay*. London: Sage.

————. 2006b. The business of making digital games. In *Understanding digital games*, ed. Jason Rutter and Jo Bryce, 36–57. London: Sage.

Kerr, Aphra, and Roddy Flynn. 2003. Revisiting globalisation through the movie and digital games industries. *Convergence: The Journal of Research into New Media Technologies* 9(1):91–113.

Kim, Alex. 2007. Time to set standard of online gaming. *Korea Times*, February 26, 2007.

Kim, Chang Duck, and Buhm Suck Kim. 2009. National represent game company NCsoft. *Dong-a Ilbo*, June 27, 2009.

Kim, Dong Won. 2005. Power of cultural content. *Digital Times*, August 2, 2005.

Kim, Doo Young. 2006. Hanaro, share the Wireline Telecom with KT. *Dong-A Ilbo*, January 2, 2006, 38.

Kim, Jae Sup. 2008. High-speed Internet firms stop telemarketing. *Hangaerae Shinmun* 12(May):16.

Kim, Joo Han, Yoon Mi Lee, Min Gyu Kim, and Eun Joo Kim. 2006. A study on the factors and types of on-line game addiction: An application of the self-determination Theory. *Journal of Korean Communication* 50(5):79–107.

Kim, Joo Hyun. 2005. Pro game wind, now eSports. *Kyunghwang Shinmun*, May 13, 2005.

Kim, Jun Il. 2005. *Lineage*: The prince of online gaming. *Kyunghyang Shinmun*, December 12, 2005.

Kim, Min Hee. 2005. Korea to nurture software industry. *Korea Herald*, December 2, 2005.

Kim, Min Kyu. 2005. SKT Lim Yo-Hwan, for three years he could get $780,000. *Omynews*, April 17, 2005.

Kim, Pyung Ho. 2006. Is Korea a strong Internet nation? *Information Society* 22:41–44.

Kim, Sung Mi. 2004. Companies revel in product placement. *Korea Herald*, September 6, 2004.

Kim, Tae Gye. 2005. Pro gamers save KTF W 46 Billion. *Korea Times*, January 2, 2005.

Kim, Tong Hyung. 2009. Online game publishers rolling in tough times. *Korea Times.* May 4, 2009.

Kline, Stephen, Nick Dyer-Witheford, and Greig de Peuter. 2003. *Digital play: The interaction of technology, culture, and marketing.* Montreal: McGill-Queen's University Press.

Kolar-Panov, D. 1996. Video and the diasporic imagination of selfhood: A case study of the Croatians in Australia. *Cultural Studies* 10(2):288–314.

Korea Communications Commission. 2009. High-speed Internet subscribers in April 2009. Available at http://www.kcc.go.kr/tsi/etc/search/search/ASC _integrationsearch.jsp

Korea Creative Content Agency. 2009. *2009 Korea game whitepaper.* Seoul: Korea Creative Content Agency.

Korea e-Sports Association. 2008a. E-Sports biz in Korea. Available at http:// www.e-sports.or.kr

Korea e-Sports Association. 2008b. E-Sports information. Available at http:// www.e-sports.or.kr

Korea e-Sports Association. 2008c. What is eSports? Available at http://www .e-sports.or.kr/esports/esports_intro_10.kea?m_code=espor_10

Korea e-Sports Association. 2009. What is eSports? Available at http://www .e-sports.or.kr/

Korea Game Industry Agency. 2006. *2006 Korean game whitepaper.* Seoul: Korea Game Industry Agency.

Korea Game Industry Agency. 2007a. *2007 Korean game whitepaper.* Seoul: Korea Game Industry Agency.

Korea Game Industry Agency. 2007b. G-Star 2007 opens. Press release, November 7, 2007.

Korea Game Industry Agency. 2008. *2008 Korean game whitepaper.* Seoul: Korea Game Industry Agency.

Korea Herald. 1999. Korean venture firm acquires U.S. game network developer, November 25, 1999.

Korea Herald. 2000. *Lineage* game popular in Taiwan, September 21, 2000.

Korean Film Council. 2009. *Korea film yearbook 2008.* Seoul: Koefic.

Korean Game Industry Agency. 2008. About KOGIA. Available at http://www .gameinfinity.or.kr/english/about_kgdi/03history.jsp

Korea Press Foundation. 2005. *Korean media yearbook 2005/2006.* Seoul: Korea Press Foundation.

Korea Stock Exchange. 2002. 2002 share-ownership in Korea. Press release, December 29, 2002.

Korea Stock Market Company. 1999. *KOSPI trend,* December 5, 1999.

Korea Times. 2001. Investor confidence in Bourse lower than in late 1998, April 11, 2001.

Korea Times. 2002. KT seeks to mitigate investor concern following privatization, May 7, 2002.

Korea Times. 2003 Asian online game providers rush to Nasdaq, December 23, 2003.

Korea Times. 2007. *Lineage* set to land in Philippines, February 13, 2007.

Kotz, David M. 2002. Globalization and neoliberalism. *Rethinking Marxism* 14(1):64–79.

Krippner, Greta R. 2005. The financialization of the American economy. *Socio-Economic Review* 3(2):173–208.

Ku, Dong Hae. 2007. Wealth and respect: Korea is a heaven of pro gamers. *Seoul Shinmun,* July 2, 2007.

Kucklich, Julian. 2005. Precarious playbour: Modders and the digital games industry. *Fibreculture* 5. Available at http:journal.fibreculture.org/issue5/index .html

Kwon, Ki Duk. 2006. How to stay ahead as digital powerhouse. *Korea Herald,* February 23, 2006.

Kwon, Oh Young. 2007. NCsoft 10 years by numbers: The global myth. *Kyunghyang Shinmun,* April 4, 2007.

KyungHyung Shinmun. 2002. The Korean economy: High-speed Internet, December 27, 2002.

Lafferty, Michael. 2007. North American producer Adam Davidson talks about *Lineage II*'s 5th Chronicle. Available at http://lineage2.mmoabc.com/ articleview/5.html

Larson, James F., and Heung-Soo Park. 1993. *Global television and the politics of the Seoul Olympics.* Boulder, Colo.: Westview Press.

Lau, Tuen Yu, Si-wook Kim, and David Atkin. 2005. An examination of factors contributing to South Korea's global leadership in broadband adoption. *Telematics and Informatics* 22(4):349–359.

Lazzarato, Maurizio. 1996. Immaterial labour. Available at http://geocities.com/ immateriallabour/lazzarato-immaterial-labour.html

Lee, David. 2006. Online gaming becoming part of life. *Korea Times,* October 8, 2006.

Lee, Dong-hoo. 2004. Cultural contact with Japanese TV dramas: modes of reception and narrative transparency. In *Feeling Asian modernities: Transnational consumption of Japanese TV dramas,* ed. Koichi Iwabuchi, 251-274. Hong Kong: Hong Kong University Press.

Lee, E. V., and S. S. Ryu. 2006. Information technology industry forecast: Contents. *Information Technology Industry Forecast* 12:245–277.

Lee, Hee Jin, Sang Jo Oh, and Yong Woon Shim. 2005. Do we need broadband? Impacts of broadband in Korea. *Info: The journal of policy, regulation, and strategy for telecommunications, information and media* 7(4):47–56.

Lee, Hee Jin, Robert M. O'Keefe, and Kyoung Lim Yun. 2003. The growth of broadband and electronic commerce in South Korea: Contributing factors. *Information Society* 19(1):81–93.

Lee, Jong Suk. 2000. *Balanced cultural policy*. Available at http://www.kcpi .or.kr/database/e_sosik/20000102/news_1.html

Lee, Joo Young. 2008. IP-cable TV competition in full swing. *Kyunghwang Shinmun*. December 26, 2008, 14.

Lee, Na-ree. 2009. Wow, AION. *Joongang Ilbo*, January 8, 2009.

Lee, Sung Hee. 2009. Special Force Pro League promotes clan and fan club. *Betanews*, May 11, 2009. Available at http://www.betanews.net/print/455291

Lee, Sungjoo, Moon-Soo Kim, and Park Yongtae. 2009. ICT co-evolution and Korean ICT strategy—An analysis based on patent data. *Telecommunications Policy* 33(5/6):253–271.

Lee, Taek Soo. 2007. CJ, game team PR effects $13.2 million. *Digital Times*, April 5, 2007.

Lee, Tak-soo. 2006. eSport market size $40 million. *Digital Times*, December 28, 2006.

Lee, Yong Kyung, and Dong Myn Lee. 2003. Broadband access in Korea: Experience and future perspective. *IEEE Communications Magazine* 41(12):30–36.

Leonard, David. 2006. An untapped field: Exploring the world of virtual sports gaming. In *Handbook of sports and media*, ed. Arthur A. Raney and Jennings Bryant, 393–407. Mahwah, N.J.: Lawrence Erlbaum.

Letto-Gillies, Grazia. 2005. *Transnational corporation and international production: Concepts, theories, and effects*. Cheltenham: Edward Elgar Publishing.

Lim, Hang. 2001. Hype of education information policy. *Kookmin Ilbo*, April 25, 2001, 3.

Lim, Yo-Hwan. 2007. *Crazy like me*. Seoul: Bookroad.

Lines, Gill. 2000. Media sport audiences-young people and the Summer of Sport '96: Revisiting frameworks for analysis. *Media Culture & Society* 22(5):669–680.

Livingstone, Sonia. 2003. The changing nature of audiences: From the mass audience to the interactive media user. In *A companion to media studies*, ed. Angharad N. Valdivia, 337–359. Oxford: Blackwell.

Macintyre, Donald. 2000. Online gaming; Web warriors: Have fingers, will fight. *Time Asia* 156(23), December 11, 2000. Available at Gaminghttp://www.time .com/time/asia/magazine/2000/1211/cover1_sb1.html

Malaby, Thomas. 2006. Parlaying value: Capital in and beyond virtual worlds. *Games and Culture* 1(2):141–162.

Martinsons, Maris G. 2005. Online games transform leisure time for young Chinese. *Communications of the ACM* 48(4):51.

Marx, Karl. 1867. The mystery of the fetishistic character of commodities. In *Communication and class struggle: Capitalism, imperialism*, ed. Armand Mattelart and Seth Siegelaub, 80–84. New York and Bagnolet: International General/ IMMRC.

Mato, Daniel. 2005. The transnationalization of the Telenovela industry, territorial references, and the production of markets and representations of transnational identities. *Television and New Media* 6(4):423–444.

McAllister, Ken S. 2004. *Game work: Language, power, and computer game culture.* Tuscaloosa: The University of Alabama Press.

McChesney, Robert. 1999. *Rich media, poor democracy.* Urbana: University of Illinois Press.

———. 2000. The political economy of communication and the future of the field. *Media Culture & Society* 22(1):109–116.

———. 2008. *The political economy of media: Enduring issues, emerging dilemmas.* New York: Monthly Review Press.

McCormack, Mike. 2007. Customising is key to Asia for *Grand Theft Auto*'s successor, July 22, 2007. Available at http://business.scotsman.com/6983/ Customising-is-key-to-Asia.3308963.jp?CommentPage=1&CommentPage Length=1000

McCrea, Christian. 2009. Watching *StarCraft*, strategy and South Korea. In *Gaming cultures and place in Asia-Pacific*, ed. Larisa Hjorth and Dean Chan, 179–212. London: Routledge.

McFadyen, Stuart, Colin Hoskins, and Adam Finn. 1998. The effect of cultural differences on the international co-production of television programs and feature films. *Canadian Journal of Communication* 23(4):523–538.

McRobbie, A. 2002. From Holloway to Hollywood: Happiness at work in the new cultural economy. In *Cultural economy: Cultural analysis and commercial life*, ed. P. Du Gay and M. Pryke, 97–114. London: Sage.

Media Future Institute. 2007. Future of platform in the convergence era between broadcasting and telecommunication. *Media plus Future*, July 2007.

Meehan, Eileen. 1993. Commodity audience, actual audience: The blindspot debate. In *Illuminating the blindspots,* ed. Janet Wasco, Vincent Mosco, and Manjunath Pendakur, 378-400. Norwood, N.J.: Ablex.

Mesthene, Emmanuel G. 1970. *Technological Change.* New York: Signet.

MGame. 2009. About MGame. Available at http://www.mgamecorp.com/main .php

Miege, Bernard. 1989. *The capitalization of cultural production.* New York: International General.

Mikoishi. 2007. Former MTV CEO and EA vice president to join Mikoishi. Press release, July 26, 2007. Available at http://www.mikoishi.com/news_ea _mtv.htm

Miller, Daniel, and Don Slater. 2000. *The Internet: An ethnographic approach.* Oxford: Berg.

Miller, Toby. 2006. Gaming for beginners. *Games and Culture* 1(1):5–12.

Ministry of Culture and Tourism. 2006. Game industry policy exhibition. Press release, February 10, 2006.

Ministry of Information and Communication. 2002 White Paper on Information and Communication In Korea, Seoul: MIC.

Ministry of Information and Communication. 2004. *Broadband IT Korea vision 2007*. Seoul: Ministry of Information and Communication.

Ministry of Information and Communication. 2006. *Survey on information-oriented status*. Seoul: Ministry of Information and Communication.

MMmogchart.com. 2007. MMOG active subscribers version 21. Available at http://www.mmogchart.com.

Mosco, Vincent. 1996. *The political economy of communication*. London: Sage.

Mosco, Vincent. 2009a. *The political economy of communication*. 2nd ed. London: Sage.

Mosco, Vincent. 2009b. Knowledge workers of the world! Unite? *Communication, Culture, Critique* 1(1):105–115.

Murdock, Graham, and Peter Golding. 1997. For a political economy of mass communication. In *The political economy of the media*, ed. Peter Golding and Graham Murdoch, 3–50. Cheltenham: Edward Elgar.

Naeil News. 2009. High-speed Internet corporations compete to upgrade speed. April 15, 2009.

Nakamura, Lisa. 2009. Don't hate the play, hate the game: The racialization of labor in *World of Warcraft*. *Critical Studies in Media Communication* 26(2):128–144.

NCsoft. 2007a. Company history: At the forefront of line games Available at http://www.ncsoft.com/kor/nccompany/history.asp

NCsoft. 2007b. Global network. Available at http://www.ncsoft.net/global/aboutus/globalnetwork.aspx?office=NAI

NCsoft. 2009a. Investor relations, 2004-2009. Available at http://www.ncsoft.net/global/ir/earnings.aspx?BID=&BC=2009

NCsoft. 2009b. NCsoft. Available at http://www.ncsoft.net/korean/download/CompanyOverview_NCsoft_KOR.pdf

Neff, Gina, Elizabeth Wissinger, and Sharon Zukin. 2005. Entrepreneurial labor among cultural producers: "Cool" jobs in "hot" industries. *Social Semiotics* 15(3):307–334.

Nikkei Weekly. 2003. Shanda buys into Japan firm making game software, June 2, 2003.

Nikunen, Kaarina. 2007. The intermedial practises of fandom. *Nordicom Review* 28(2):111–128.

Nordenstreng, Kaarle, and Tapio Varis. 1974. *Television traffic a one-way street: A survey and analysis of the international flow of television programme material*. Paris: UNESCO.

Number of Fan Club Members. Available at http://ww.daum.net.

Oh, Sung Wan. 2007. Onmedia, join the game industry. *Naeil News*, March 6, 2007.

Olsen, J. and J. Zinner. 2001. Game developer's salary survey. Gamasutra, August 31, 2001.

Ongamenet. 2008. Business info. Available at http://www.onmedia.co.kr

Organization for Economic Co-operation and Development. 2008. OECD broadband portal. Available at http://www.oecd.org/sti/ict/broadband

Pacey, Arnold. 1983. *The culture of technology*. Cambridge, Mass.: MIT Press.

Park, Dong Whee. 2008. Production cost $10 million era. *HanKyung Daily*, September 21, 2008.

Park, H. C. 2006. Go to the scene of e-sports. *Hangarae Shinmun*, September 11, 2006.

Park, Myung Ki. 2008. There is a feast everyday in Blizzard, *Daily Sports*, May 5, 2008.

Park, Nam Ki. 2006. U.S. cable broadcasters expand their investment to the game industry. *Foreign Broadcasting Information* July:67–69.

Parks Associates. 2005. Taiwan and Korea lead in the adoption of consumer technologies. Press release, November 21, 2005.

Pedersen, Isabel. 2008. No Apple iPhone? You must be Canadian: Mobile technologies, participatory culture, and rhetorical transformation. *Canadian Journal of Communication* 33:491–510.

Postigo, Hector. 2003. From Pong to Planet Quake: Post industrial transitions from leisure to work. *Information Communication and Society* 6(4):593–607.

Preston, Paschal, and Aphra Kerr. 2001. Digital media, nation-states and local cultures: the case of multimedia "content" production. *Media Culture & Society* 23(1):109–131.

PriceWaterHouse Coopers. 2006. *Global entertainment and media outlook 2006-2010*.

PriceWaterHouse Coopers. 2007. *Global entertainment and media outlook 2007-2011*.

PriceWaterHouse Coopers. 2008. *Global entertainment and media outlook 2008-2012*.

Raessens, Joost. 2005. Computer games as participatory media culture. In *Handbook of computer game studies*, ed. Joost Raessens and Jeffrey Goldstein, 373–388. Cambridge, Mass.: MIT Press.

Ramstad, Evan. 2006. South Korea's NHN, joining U.S. market, plans game Web site. *Wall Street Journal*, July 26, 2006, D10.

Rescher, Nicholas. 1969. What is value change? A framework for research. In *Values and the future*, ed. Kurt Baier and Nicholas Rescher, 12–44. New York: The Free Press.

Reynolds, Taylor, and Sacks, Gary. 2003. Promoting broadband: Background paper.

Rhee, So-eui, and Michael Wei. 2009. China bids for Asia online game crown against Korea. Reuters.

Rodriguez, Hector. 2006. The Playful and the Serious: An approximation to Huizinga's Homo Ludens. Game Studies. 6(1) Available at http://gamestudies .org/0601/articles/rodriges

Rohwer, Jim. 2000. The new Net Tigers: Korea. *Fortune* 15:310–318.

Rohwer, Jim, Neel Chowdhury, and Louis Kraar. 2000. The new Net Tigers: Three years ago, the Asian Tigers were written off for dead. Now three of them—South Korea, Taiwan, and Hong Kong—have embraced the Internet and are on a tear. Could this be the key to Asia's recovery. *Fortune* 15(May), 310–318.

Rowe, David. 1996. The global love-match: Sport and television. *Media Culture & Society* 18(4):565–582.

———. 2004. *Sport, culture and the media.* 2nd ed. New York: Open University Press.

Ryoo, Sun Sil. 2008. M&A in the domestic game industry. *Information and Telecommunications Policy* 20(4):43–45.

Ryoo, Woong Jae. 2009. Globalization, or the logic of cultural hybridization: the case of the Korean Wave. *Asian Journal of Communication* 19(2):137–151.

Ryu, Seoung Ho. 2008. Unlocking the positive potential of video games. *Korea Herald*, September 1, 2008.

Samsung Economic Research Institute. 2005a. *Issue paper: The current status of e-Sport and its development strategy.* Seoul: Samsung Economic Research Institute.

Samsung Economic Research Institute. 2005b. *CEO information 520.* Seoul: Samsung Economic Research Institute.

SBS. 2008. Game show, amusing world. Available at http://tv.sbs.co.kr/ gameshow

Scherer, Jay. 2007. Globalization, promotional culture and the production/consumption of online games: Engaging Adidas's Beat Rugby campaign. *New Media & Society* 9(3):475–496.

Schiesel, Seth. 2006. The land of the video geek. *New York Times*, October 8, 2006, C1.

Schiller, Dan. 1996. *Theorizing communication: A history.* New York: Oxford University Press.

———. 2000. *Digital capitalism: Networking the global market system.* Cambridge, Mass.: MIT Press.

———. 2007. *How to think about information.* Urbana, Ill.: University of Illinois Press.

Schiller, Herbert. 1976. *Communication and cultural dominance.* New York: International Arts and Sciences Press.

Seo, Sung Kon. 2009. Game industry Big Five surpasses sale of 2 billion. *inews.* May 19, 2009.

Seong, Nak Yang. 2006. How has Korea become Internet powerhouse? *Korea Times,* September 22, 2006.

Sepstrup, Preben. 1990. *Transnationalization of television in Western Europe.* London: John Libbey and Co.

Shanda. 2007. Shanda to operate TECMO's flagship game, dead or alive online. Press release, July 2, 2007. Available at http://www.snda.com/en/news/news .jsp?id=451

Shefrin, Elana. 2004. Lord of Rings, Star Wars, and participatory fandom: Mapping new congruencies between the Internet and media entertainment culture. *Critical Studies in Media Communication* 21(3) (:261–281.

Shim, Hwa Yong. 2008. Sony-Nintendo compete in Korea. *Digital Times,* March 15, 2008.

Shim, M. K. 2009. Bluestudio develops TERA. *Asian Today,* January 23, 2009.

Shimpach, Shawn. 2005. Working watching: The creative and cultural labor of the media audience. *Social Semiotics* 15(3):343–360.

Shome, Raka, and Radha Hedge. 2002. Culture, communication, and the challenge of globalization. *Critical Studies in Media Communication* 19(2):172–189.

Sinclair, John, and Mark Harrison. 2004. Globalization, nation, and television in Asia: The case of India and China. *Television and New Media* 5(1):41–54.

Siriyuvasak, Ubonrat, and Hyun-joon Shin. 2007. Asianizing K-POP: Production, consumption and identification patterns among Thai youth. *Inter-Asia Cultural Studies* 8(1):109–136.

SK Broadband. 2008. SK Broadband provides online game AION package service. Press release, November 11, 2008.

Smythe, Dallas. 1951. The consumer's stake in radio and television. *Caliber: Quarterly of Film Radio and Television* 4:109–128.

———. 1977. Communication: Blindspot of western Marxism. *Canadian Journal of Political and Social Theory* 1(3):1–27.

———. 1981. *Dependency road.* Norwood, N.J.: Ablex.

Smythe, Dallas, and Thomas Guback. 1994. *Counterclockwise: Perspectives on communication.* Boulder: Westview.

Song, Jung A. 2004. South Korea top for online gaming: The country's market is expected to grow $45 this year, with NCsoft leading the charge. *Financial Times,* December 31, 2004, 19.

Starbase. 2008. Condition for the growth of in-game ads. June 16, 2008.

Sterling, Bruce. 2005. Typing into the abyss. Paper presented at the International Communication Conference Association. New York.

Strategy Analytics. 2009. US ranks 20th in global broadband household penetration. Press release, June 18, 2009.

Suhr, Hiesun Cecilia. 2009. Underpinning the paradoxes in the artistic fields of MySpace: The problematization of values and popularity in convergence culture. *New Media & Society* 11(172):179–198.

Surowiecki, James. 2004. *The wisdom of crowds*. New York: Doubleday.

Taylor, Chris. 2006. The future is in South Korea. *CNN Money*. Available at http://money.cnn.com/2006/06/08/technology/business2_futureboy0608/index .htm

Terranova, Tiziana. 2000. Free labor: Producing culture for the digital economy. *Social Text* 18(2):33–58.

Terranova, Tiziana. 2004. *Network culture: Politics for the information age*. New York, N.Y.: Pluto Press.

Theberge, Paul. 2005. Everyday fandom: Fan clubs, blogging, and the quotidian rhythms of the Internet. *Canadian Journal of Communication* 30(4):485–502.

This is Game.Com. 2009. Average annual salary of game workers in the U.S. game firms makes two or three times higher than that of Korean workers. Available at http://www.thisisgame.com/board/view.php?id=236000&category =117

Thussu, Daya K. 2006a. *International communication: Continuity and change*. 2nd ed. London: Arnold.

———. 2006b. Mapping global flow and contra-flow. In *Media on the move: global flow and contra-flow*, ed. Daya Thussu, 11–32. London: Routledge.

Tomlinson, John. 1999. *Globalization and culture*. Chicago: The University of Chicago.

Tufte, Thomas. 1995. How to telenovelas serve to articulate hybrid cultures in contemporary Brazil? *Nordicom Review* 2:29–35.

Twin Galaxies. 2004. About our history. Available at http://www.twingalaxies .com/index.aspx?c=17&id=332

Wagner, Michael G. 2006. On the scientific relevance of eSports. International Conference on Internet Computing 2006, June 26–29, 2006, Las Vegas, Nevada.

Wallace, Bruce. 2007. Gamer is royalty in S. Korea. *Los Angeles Times*. March 21, 2007.

Wallerstein, Immanuel. 1974. *The modern world-system: Capitalist agriculture and the origins of the European world-economy in the sixteenth century*. New York: Academic Press.

Wang, Georgette, and Emilie Yueh-Yu Yeh. 2005. Globalization and hybridization in cultural products: The cases of Mulan and Crouching Tiger, Hidden Dragon. *International Journal of Cultural Studies* 8(2):175–193.

Ward, Andrew. 2004. Where high-speed access is going mainstream the Korean experience: Government policy, high levels of urbanization. *Financial Times*, June 9, 2004, 4.

Wark, Mckenzie. 2007. *Gamer theory*. Cambridge, Mass.: Harvard University Press.

Wasko, Janet. 1994. *Hollywood in the information age*. Cambridge: Polity Press.

Wasser, Frederick. 1995. Is Hollywood America? The transnationalization of the American film industry. *Critical Studies in Media Communication* 12:423–437.

Webster, Frank. 2002. *Theories of the information society*. 2nd ed. London: Routledge.

Wemade. 2007. About Wemade. Available at http://www.wemade.com/main/main.asp

Whang, Hee Tae. 2006. Gloomy domestic game firms before EC. *Saegae Ilbo*, 12.

Whang, Leo Sang-Min. 2003. Online game dynamics in Korean society: Experiences and lifestyles in the online game world. *Korea Journal* 43(3):7–34.

Williams, Raymond. 1974. *Television: Technology and cultural form*. London: Routledge.

Williams, Raymond. 1992. *Television: Technology and cultural form*. London: Wesleyan University Press.

Wolf, Mark J. 2002. *The medium of video game*. 2nd ed. Austin: University of Texas Press.

Wolf, Mark J., and Bernard Perron, ed. 2003. *The video game theory reader*. New York: Routledge.

World Cyber Games. 2008. Statistics. Available at http://www.wcg.com/6th/2008/tournament/statistics_overview.asp

Games, World Cyber. 2009. Statistics. Available at http://www.wcg.com/6th/history/wcg2009/wcg2009_overview_kr.asp

Wu, Huaiting, and Joseph M. Chan. 2007. Globalizing Chinese martial arts cinema: The global-local alliance and the production of Crouching Tiger, Hidden Dragon. *Media Culture & Society* 29(2):195–217.

Yang, Li. 2007. EA grows online gaming footprint in Asia, May 22, 2007. Available at http://www.cctv.com/program/bizchina/20070522/105283.shtml

Yang, Sung Jin. 2009. CJ Group takes over OnMedia. *Korea Herald*, 25 December.

Yang, Sung Jin. 2003. NCsoft enters China's online game market with *Lineage*. *Korea Herald*, January 12, 2003, 31.

Yee, Nick. 2006a. The labor of fun: How video games blur the boundaries of work and play. *Games and Culture* 1(1):68–71.

———. 2006b. The demographics, motivations, and derived experiences of users of massively multi-user online graphical environments. *Presence (Cambridge, Mass.)* 15(2):309–329.

Yi, In Hwa. 2006. Korea, the everlasting empire in the online world. *JoongAng Ilbo*, July 21, 2006.

Yonhap News. 2002. The decrease in female pro-gamers, January 9, 2002.

Yoon, A Rum. 2005. Game fans 32% want eSports military team. *KyungHwang Games,* November 14, 2005.

Yoon, Kyung Won. 2006. The making of neo-Confucian cyberkids: Representations of young mobile phone users in South Korea. *New Media & Society* 8(5):753–771.

You, Soh Jung. 2003. *Lineage* creates second cyberworld living space. *Korea Herald.* 8:40.

Index